11+ COMPREHENSION: MULTIPLE CHOICE, VOLUME 2

In-Depth Guided Explanations

MIRANDA MATTHEWS

Copyright © 2021 Accolade Tuition Ltd
Published by Accolade Tuition Ltd
71-75 Shelton Street
Covent Garden
London WC2H 9JQ
www.accoladetuition.com
info@accoladetuition.com

The right of Miranda Matthews to be identified as the author of this work has been asserted by her in accordance with the Copyright, Designs and Patents Act 1988.

All rights reserved. No part of this book may be reproduced in any form or by any electronic or mechanical means, including information storage and retrieval systems, without written permission from the author, except for the use of brief quotations in a book review.

ISBN 978-1-913988-23-4

FIRST EDITION

1 3 5 7 9 10 8 6 4 2

Contents

Note on Volume 2   v
Editor's Foreword   vii

The Scattershot Paper

Paper One: Agnes Grey   3
Paper One: Answers & Guidance   13
Paper Two: The Young Fur Traders   29
Paper Two: Answers & Guidance   39

The Three-Parter Paper

Paper Three: The Secret Garden   55
Paper Three: Answers & Guidance   65
Paper Four: Sea and Sardinia   81
Paper Four: Answers & Guidance   91

The Poetry Paper

Paper Five: On A Spaniel Called Beau   107
Paper Five: Answers & Guidance   111
Paper Six: The Cat and the Moon   117
Paper Six: Answers & Guidance   121

The Extended Concentration Paper

Paper Seven: Clayhanger   129
Paper Seven: Answers & Guidance   143
Paper Eight: The Mill on the Floss   165
Paper Eight: Answers & Guidance   179

Afterword   201
Accolade Press for Entrance Exams   203
Accolade Press for Key Stage 2 & 3   205
Accolade Press for GCSE English: The Range   207

Note on Volume 2

Welcome to Accolade's second volume of 11+ multiple choice comprehension papers.

The foreword that follows this note is largely unchanged from the foreword that appeared in the first volume, and contains all of the same "general" advice and guidance. Moreover, the way this book is structured is also much the same: eight papers, split into four subcategories (as explained in more depth in the foreword). However, each of the eight papers are wholly original. And while the explanations to some answers do repeat some of the guidance that appears in Volume 1, all explanations are of course tailored to the wholly original exam papers in this guide.

Editor's Foreword

When sitting 11+ comprehension exams at top schools (be they independent powerhouses, or high-flying grammars) you will notice that, although all of their papers follow the basic formula – an extract accompanied by a set of questions – the *types* of questions they ask can vary greatly. The reason for this is simple enough: a considerable number of these schools write their papers in-house, and that means you find quirks in some papers that you don't in others. Even papers produced by examining bodies, such as the CEM and GL papers, have their idiosyncrasies. And yet, for all these quirks, there is still a *huge* degree of overlap between these various papers, because ultimately these schools are all looking for a similar set of skills.

As a result, preparing for these exams is eminently possible. We simply need to familiarize ourselves with the various types of multiple-choice questions that appear (including those quirky ones!), then hone the skills required to answer them.

The intention of this guide is not simply to show you what these exams tend to look like (although, as you work through it, you will inevitably get a sense of this nonetheless!). No, the intention is to go a step further, and show you how to decode the sorts of questions these 11+ comprehension papers tend to ask, and how to go about deducing the answer.

Now, before we press on, I feel it is important to make one crucial thing clear: this guide is explicitly aimed at those students looking to achieve at the very highest level. This guide on multiple occasions makes use of sophisticated vocabulary and ideas. I promise you that the intention is *not* to intimidate. Rather, we must remember that these are competitive exams, and so it is imperative that we give ourselves the very best chance to succeed.

Rest assured, however, that when these tricky words or phrases are used, they are also accompanied by detailed explanations. As a result, by the time you finish working through this guide, you should have a whole new arsenal of words and phrases to help you attack papers of any kind!

How This Book Is Set Out

As mentioned, 11+ papers are incredibly varied. However, if you spend enough time and energy looking through past papers, you start to figure out what makes them tick, and notice certain patterns that emerge time and again. This book contains eight papers that have been split into four different "styles" of questioning – two papers for each style. I have labelled the four types of papers as follows:

1. The Scattershot Paper
2. The Three-Parter Paper
3. The Poetry Paper
4. The Extended Concentration Paper

The labels I've given each style should give you some indication of what the papers entail. It may well be the case that some of the 11+ comprehension papers you end up taking fit neatly into the one of these styles. However, it is just as possible that they wind up being a blend of two (or more) styles – after all, schools often tweak the style of paper they put out year on year. At any rate, I can assert with confidence that, if you are well versed in all four styles, you will have your bases covered, and be prepared for most anything.

The questions for each paper appear twice. The first time they will appear is immediately after the extract, so that students can, if they wish, have a go at tackling the paper. They will then appear a second time, but this time accompanied by the correct answers and detailed guidance.

Each of the papers includes a "time guide" – that is, the amount of time one would expect to be given to complete the paper in an exam hall. If students wish to complete some of these papers as practice, I suspect this may prove useful.

Insofar as difficulty is concerned, the first paper in each style might be described as "difficult," and the second "devilish." Again, I feel the need to reiterate that the intention is *not* to intimidate. On the contrary, by exposing students to the reality of what is in store, I believe it ensures that, when it actually comes to entering the exam hall, you feel far more at ease.

There is no *correct* way to use this guide. Some students will feel comfortable working through it by themselves, whereas some may prefer to have a parent at hand to act as a kind of surrogate tutor. In any case, the intention of this book is to give the reader the experience of having an experienced tutor at their beck and call.

Exam Tips

Within this book, you will find a good deal of question specific advice. However, there are a number of more general tips that it is important for any 11+ candidate to keep in mind:

- When reading the extract, don't rush. Some papers even set aside 10 minutes explicitly for reading the paper, and do not allow you to look at the questions until those 10 minutes have elapsed. This does not mean that 10 minutes is always necessary – but keep in mind that every school will expect you to read the passage very carefully.
- Read the questions carefully. It sounds obvious, I know, but you wouldn't believe how many times I have seen bright students lose marks simply because they have misread the question.
- If the question is asking you the meaning of a certain word or phrase, always go back and read that word or phrase in context. Remember: not only does context impact on meaning, but it can also help you make an educated guess if you do not know the answer with certainty.
- Embrace the process of elimination. It's a great way to double-check that you have the correct answer when you feel you know it off the bat. Moreover, it's a great way of increasing your odds when you are unsure.
- Even if you have no idea what the correct answer is, never leave a question blank. A guess is better than a guaranteed lost mark.

Personal Note

When I talk about my academic career, I usually talk about my time spent at university: I studied English Literature & Language at UCL, then took a Masters at Cambridge University. However, a mere twenty years ago, I was in the same position that many of my readers find themselves in: eager to win a place at a top secondary school, and faced with a litany of exams. Of course, the exams have changed a fair bit since then; but what I'm trying to say is, not only have I been teaching 11+ students for many years, but I've also had firsthand experience of it – I know what it's like to live through!

Even though I now look back on that time through a rosy lens – I was offered places at all the top London private and grammar schools I sat for – I won't pretend as though it was not at times intimidating. However, I would observe that many parts of the 11+ English exams, and especially the comprehension papers, offer rare opportunities to engage with truly amazing works of literature. That is not to say that these exams are *fun* – my memory of them is pretty much the exact opposite – but still, it is important to at least try and embrace this side of things and enjoy the challenge.

The Scattershot Paper

I have labelled the two papers that follow 'scattershot papers', because the questions are not separated by 'type' into different sections; instead, all different kinds of questions – retrieval, inference, definitions – are thrown in together, which means candidates need to be constantly prepared to shift gears. Scattershot-style papers of this kind are what many private schools employ, but they also very closely resemble the GL and CEM papers.

You will notice that the questions in these scattershot papers each have four options (a, b, c, d) to pick from. Be aware, however, that some scattershot papers will have five options instead, which makes life that little bit harder. That said, we will be looking at questions with five options a little bit later in this guide.

Paper One: Agnes Grey
SCATTERSHOT PAPER; DIFFICULT; 40 MINUTES

This extract is taken from a novel published in 1847. At this early point in the book, the Grey family have lost their wealth, and the father of the family has become ill.

---

1   Through all our troubles, I never but once heard my mother complain of our want of money. As summer was coming on she observed to Mary and me, "What a desirable thing it would be for your papa to spend a few weeks at a watering-place. I am convinced the sea-air and the change of scene would be of incalculable service to
5   him. But then, you see, there's no money," she added, with a sigh. We both wished exceedingly that the thing might be done, and lamented greatly that it could not. "Well, well!" said she, "it's no use complaining. Possibly something might be done to further the project after all. Mary, you are a beautiful drawer. What do you say to doing a few more pictures in your best style, and getting them framed, with the water-
10 coloured drawings you have already done, and trying to dispose of them to some liberal picture-dealer, who has the sense to discern their merits?"

"Mamma, I should be delighted if you think they *could* be sold; and for anything worth while."

"It's worth while trying, however, my dear: do you procure the drawings, and I'll
15 endeavour to find a purchaser."

"I wish *I* could do something," said I.

"You, Agnes! well, who knows? You draw pretty well, too: if you choose some simple piece for your subject, I daresay you will be able to produce something we shall all be proud to exhibit."

"But I have another scheme in my head, mamma, and have had long, only I did not like to mention it."

"Indeed! pray tell us what it is."

"I should like to be a governess."

My mother uttered an exclamation of surprise, and laughed. My sister dropped her work in astonishment, exclaiming, "*You* a governess, Agnes! What can you be dreaming of?"

"Well! I don't see anything so *very* extraordinary in it. I do not pretend to be able to instruct great girls; but surely I could teach little ones: and I should like it so much: I am so fond of children. Do let me, mamma!"

"But, my love, you have not learned to take care of *yourself* yet: and young children require more judgment and experience to manage than elder ones."

"But, mamma, I am above eighteen, and quite able to take care of myself, and others too. You do not know half the wisdom and prudence I possess, because I have never been tried."

"Only think," said Mary, "what would you do in a house full of strangers, without me or mamma to speak and act for you—with a parcel of children, besides yourself, to attend to; and no one to look to for advice? You would not even know what clothes to put on."

"You think, because I always do as you bid me, I have no judgment of my own: but only try me—that is all I ask—and you shall see what I can do."

At that moment my father entered and the subject of our discussion was explained to him.

"What, my little Agnes a governess!" cried he, and, in spite of his dejection, he laughed at the idea.

"Yes, papa, don't *you* say anything against it: I should like it so much; and I am sure I could manage delightfully."

"But, my darling, we could not spare you." And a tear glistened in his eye as he added—"No, no! afflicted as we are, surely we are not brought to that pass yet."

"Oh, no!" said my mother. "There is no necessity whatever for such a step; it is merely a whim of her own. So you must hold your tongue, you naughty girl; for, though you are so ready to leave us, you know very well we cannot part with *you*."

I was silenced for that day, and for many succeeding ones; but still I did not wholly relinquish my darling scheme. Mary got her drawing materials, and steadily set to work. I got mine too; but while I drew, I thought of other things. How delightful it would be to be a governess! To go out into the world; to enter upon a new life; to act for myself; to exercise my unused faculties; to try my unknown powers; to earn my own maintenance, and something to comfort and help my father, mother, and sister, besides exonerating them from the provision of my food and clothing; to show papa what his little Agnes could do; to convince mamma and Mary that I was not quite the helpless, thoughtless being they supposed. And then, how charming to be entrusted with the care and education of children! Whatever others said, I felt I was fully competent to the task: the clear remembrance of my own thoughts in early childhood would be a surer guide than the instructions of the most mature adviser. I had but to turn from my little pupils to myself at their age, and I should know, at once, how to win their confidence and affections: how to waken the contrition of the erring; how to embolden the timid and console the afflicted; how to make Virtue practicable, Instruction desirable, and Religion lovely and comprehensible.

An extract from Agnes Grey by Anne Bronte

Q1. What time of year does this excerpt take place?

a) The end of summer
b) January
c) The beginning of summer
d) During a very cold winter

Answer: ___

Q2. What does the word "lamented" in line 6 mean?

a) Laughed happily
b) Spoke sadly
c) Failed to understand
d) Shouted angrily

Answer: ___

Q3. How did the narrator's mother react to the challenge of affording a holiday for her husband?

a) With disappointment that it couldn't be done
b) With a "don't care" attitude
c) By pretending they had enough money to afford it
d) By rising to the challenge and suggesting ideas

Answer: ___

Q4. What was the meaning of a "watering-place" in line 3?

a) A place for wild animals to gather and drink
b) A place to fetch water for the household
c) A spa or seaside resort for ill or frail patients
d) A hotel with a swimming pool

Answer: ___

Q5. How was Mary asked to help the family finances?

a) By selling her drawings and watercolours
b) By working as a picture dealer
c) By becoming a governess
d) By learning to draw and paint

Answer: ___

Q6. What does "incalculable" mean in line 4?

a) Unpleasant
b) Unimportant
c) Too small to be estimated
d) Too great to be calculated

Answer: ___

Q7. How keen is Agnes, the narrator of the novel, to help with the family finances?

a) She is very keen to help
b) She is not at all keen to help
c) She is angry at the idea of helping
d) She is not keen at first, but changes her mind

Answer: ___

Q8. What is Agnes' plan to help her family?

a) To sell her artwork, like her sister
b) To care for her father at home
c) To become a governess
d) She doesn't want to work at all

Answer: ___

Q9. How do her mother and sister react to Agnes' plan for her career?

a) With whole-hearted enthusiasm
b) With disgust and disapproval
c) With anger and shouting
d) With disbelief and laughter

Answer: ___

Q10. What does the word "prudence" mean in line 33?

a) Great wealth
b) Carefulness and good sense
c) Silly childishness
d) Lack of experience

Answer: ___

Q11. How old is the narrator, Agnes?

a) Under eighteen
b) Older than eighteen
c) Still a young child
d) In her late thirties

Answer: ___

Q12. Do you think that Agnes is an obedient daughter to her parents?

a) Sometimes

b) Never
  c) When it suits her
  d) Always

Answer: ___

Q13. What type of word is "dejection"?

  a) A noun
  b) An adjective
  c) An adverb
  d) A proper noun

Answer: ___

Q14. How does Agnes' father react to her career plan?

  a) He has mixed reactions
  b) He thinks it an excellent idea
  c) He is angry with her
  d) He wants her to start immediately

Answer: ___

Q15. Does Mary believe her sister could be a governess?

  a) Yes, she is certain Agnes could do it easily
  b) No, she believes Agnes is too bad-tempered to be a governess
  c) No, she believes Agnes could not even choose appropriate clothes for the job
  d) Maybe - she wants Agnes to try it for a while and see what happens

Answer: ___

Q16. What do you think Agnes' father means when he says "Afflicted as we are"?

  a) He means the whole family is unwell
  b) The Grey family is in a feud with another family
  c) The family is disliked by the local people
  d) The family has become very poor

Answer: ___

Q17. What does the word "whim" in line 50 mean?

a) An annoying habit
b) A selfish plan
c) A sudden, odd idea
d) An impertinent question

Answer: ___

Q18. What does Agnes do about her plan to be a governess after the family dismisses it?

a) She immediately drops all her plans
b) She decides to wait five years, then try again
c) She privately continues to think about her scheme
d) She ignores her family and applies for a job immediately

Answer: ___

Q19. Why do you think Agnes describes herself as "little" when she says in line 43 "to show papa what his little Agnes could do"?

a) Because she is a very small woman
b) Because her father still thinks of her as a child, and she wants to prove him wrong
c) Because she thinks of herself as a little, helpless young woman who can't achieve much in life
d) Because she is shorter than her mother and sister

Answer: ___

Q20. How many family members do you think live in Agnes' house?

a) Five
b) Two
c) Four
d) Three

Answer: ___

Q21. What does Agnes mean when she says "Only try me" in line 40?

a) Let me have an attempt at it
b) Put me on trial
c) Annoy me and see what happens
d) Try to ignore me

Answer: ___

Q22. From line 55 (…to go out into the world…) to line 60 (…the helpless, thoughtless being they supposed.) there are seven examples of the same punctuation mark. What is it called?

a) A full stop
b) A comma
c) An exclamation mark
d) A semicolon

Answer: ___

Q23. Does Agnes remember how she felt as a child?

a) Not at all
b) Vaguely
c) Clearly
d) Occasionally

Answer: ___

Q24. What do you think "to embolden the timid" in line 66 means?

a) To make shy ones braver
b) To wake up sleepy ones
c) To make lazy ones work harder
d) To frighten the disobedient ones

Answer: ___

Q25. How do you think Agnes' family feel about her in general?

a) They do not feel very strongly about her

b) They hope she will get work and leave home
c) They feel she is a financial burden on them
d) They are loving and protective of her

Answer: ___

Paper One: Answers & Guidance

Q1. What time of year does this excerpt take place?

a) The end of summer
b) January
c) The beginning of summer
d) During a very cold winter

Answer: C

There are two key methods available to us when tackling multiple choice questions: we can either work out the correct answer outright, or we can eliminate the incorrect answers. However, it's often useful to use a **blend** of these two methods. This allows us to double-check our answers when we think we've found the correct one, but also allows us to better our odds by removing incorrect answers when we are unable to figure out the correct answer straight away.

Now, this particular question largely tests our retrieval skills – that is, our ability to comb through the extract and pick out a detail. Retrieval questions are some of the most basic questions you'll find in 11+ multi-choice comprehension papers, though that doesn't mean they can't sometimes be tricky – especially when the details are hidden in big, long paragraphs!

This question tests retrieval skills in a relatively clear manner. There is a direct reference to the time of year in the passage in the second sentence of the text (line 2) — "As summer was coming on, she observed to Mary and me..." — so we can see that **(c)** is the correct answer. If it were needed, evidence can be inferred from the subject discussed, which is a holiday with "sea air" for Agnes' father, hardly a likely idea after the summer is over, or in the winter months. So options **(a)**, **(b)** and **(d)** can be eliminated.

Q2. What does the word "lamented" in line 6 mean?

a) Laughed happily
b) Spoke sadly
c) Failed to understand
d) Shouted angrily

Answer: B

This question tests vocabulary skills, and if the word is unfamiliar, calls for gathering evidence from the surrounding text to examine which is the most likely definition.

We see that Agnes' mother is sad when she speaks, as she added a comment "with a sigh". In line 7 she says "It's no use complaining" when the sisters have just "Wished exceedingly that the thing might be done". Therefore **(b)** is the most likely answer, as **(a)** and **(c)** do not make sense, and **(d)** can be rejected as totally out of character, because of the way the girls are portrayed in this extract as helpful and good-natured.

Q3. How did the narrator's mother react to the challenge of affording a holiday for her husband?

a) With disappointment that it couldn't be done
b) With a "don't care" attitude
c) By pretending they had enough money to afford it
d) By rising to the challenge and suggesting ideas

Answer: D

A retrieval question to which the answer can be found in lines 7 to 11.

We can quickly dismiss the unlikely options of (a), (b) and (c) by seeing how Agnes' mother rises to the challenge of making money for her husband's holiday. She immediately makes plans to be able to afford this treat: "…something might be done to further the project after all" and suggests the creation and sale of her daughters' artworks. So (d) is the correct answer.

Q4. What was the meaning of a "watering-place" in line 3?

    a) A place for wild animals to gather and drink
    b) A place to fetch water for the household
    c) A spa or seaside resort for ill or frail patients
    d) A hotel with a swimming pool

Answer: C

This is a comparatively tricky vocabulary question, as there is no direct definition within the text, and the expression "watering place" has fallen out of usage in modern times.

When this novel was written in 1847, frail or recovering invalids were often advised to spend time at seaside resorts, where they not only bathed in sea water and breathed salt air (thought to be very good for the lungs and general strength) but also drank water from the local spa, which promised health-giving properties. These were known as "watering places" and were very popular with those who could afford to visit them.

So, unless the answer is already known, we must examine the options with a view to eliminating the impossible and unlikely ones.

We can firstly reject option (a) as having no relevance to the text whatsoever. Answer (b) is less obvious, but the very fact that Agnes' father would be going away from their home for his holiday implies that the Grey household water situation has nothing to do with the "watering place". Clearly, (d) is too modern an idea to fit into our current text – it would be an anachronism (something inappropriate to its surrounding time). We know from lines 2-3 that it would be a "desirable thing" for Agnes' father, who is not well, to go to this place, so the only logical answer here is option (c).

Q5. How was Mary asked to help the family finances?

a) By selling her drawings and watercolours
b) By working as a picture dealer
c) By becoming a governess
d) By learning to draw and paint

Answer: A

A more simple retrieval question here; the answer is contained in lines 8-11 when Agnes' mother says "Mary, you are a beautiful drawer. What do you say to doing a few more pictures....and trying to dispose of them to some liberal picture dealer..." so the right answer is (**a**).

Option (**b**) is a red herring, as a picture dealer is mentioned, but not as a possible job for Mary. Given the family's reaction later in the extract to the idea of Agnes leaving home, we can surely dismiss answer (**c**); and since we have read that Mary is already an accomplished artist, option (**d**) is eliminated too.

Q6. What does "incalculable" mean in line 4?

a) Unpleasant
b) Unimportant
c) Too small to be estimated
d) Too great to be calculated

Answer: D

There are several clues in this passage to help find the meaning of the word "incalculable".

That all the family wish for a healthy holiday for the father is emphasised, as in lines 2-3: "What a desirable thing it would be for your papa…"; so we can see that answers (**a**) and (**b**) can be discounted straight away.

Answer (**c**) is more difficult to reject. Some words are ambiguous, which means they might have two, or more, meanings. We have to look at the context in which "incalculable" is used here. It literally means "unable to be calculated", but since we know already that the visit to a spa town is something to be wished for "exceedingly", we

Paper One: Answers & Guidance

must eliminate answer (**c**) as being very unlikely. The remaining answer, (**d**), is therefore the right one.

Q7. How keen is Agnes, the narrator of the novel, to help with the family finances?

    a) **She is very keen to help**
    b) **She is not at all keen to help**
    c) **She is angry at the idea of helping**
    d) **She is not keen at first, but changes her mind**

Answer: A

How keen is Agnes to help with the family finances? This straightforward retrieval question can be answered by finding line 16: "I wish *I* could do something" said I." That the *I* is in italics underlines Agnes' strong desire to make a personal contribution of whatever kind necessary, so we can infer the correct answer is (**a**). Options (**b**) and (**c**) have no support in the text, and (**d**) underestimates her immediately enthusiastic response.

Q8. What is Agnes' plan to help her family?

    a) **To sell her artwork, like her sister**
    b) **To care for her father at home**
    c) **To become a governess**
    d) **She doesn't want to work at all**

Answer: C

This is a question that has the answer quite clearly in the text at line 23 when Agnes states "I should like to be a governess".

However, eliminating the other possible answers is a good idea, as answer (**a**) – by drawing and painting like her sister – has some merit too. This is the idea her mother has, and as a result of the information at line 54 – "I got [my drawing materials] too; but while I drew..." – we know Agnes did indeed do some artwork with a view to selling it. However, this is *not* what Agnes actually wanted to do, and nor was it her plan, and it is thus not the correct answer.

Moreover, we can reject option (**b**) as wrong, because caring for her father at home would not solve the family problems, while (**d**) is also incorrect, because we know Agnes is keen to work. As a result, we are left with our right answer: (**c**).

Q9. How do her mother and sister react to Agnes' plan for her career?

    a) With whole-hearted enthusiasm
    b) With disgust and disapproval
    c) With anger and shouting
    d) With disbelief and laughter

                                                        Answer: D

Here we are asked about Agnes' mother's and sister's reaction to her plan for a career. This question is a little less straightforward, as there are various reactions to Agnes' plan throughout the text, although we can see that the general reaction is a negative and unenthusiastic one. This leads us to dismiss answer (**c**) first.

Looking at option (**b**) we can perhaps say there is a slight measure of surprised disapproval in the mother and Mary's response, but there is no disgust. As for answer (**c**), there is nothing in the extract to indicate a violent reaction such as anger and shouting. So we are left to consider whether (**d**) is our best option. Examining the text, we find in line 24: "My mother uttered an exclamation of surprise, and laughed", so (**d**) is indeed correct.

Q10. What does the word "prudence" mean in line 33?

    a) Great wealth
    b) Carefulness and good sense
    c) Silly childishness
    d) Lack of experience

                                                        Answer: B

Paper One: Answers & Guidance

Another test of vocabulary which, if the word "prudence" is unknown, has to be worked out from its context within the extract.

Firstly, since Agnes is justifying herself as to her competence for the job of governess, and claims "prudence" along with "wisdom" as two appropriate and useful qualities she possesses (line 33) we can ignore answers (c) and (d) since Agnes would not be proud of these qualities. Her family believe she is childish and has no experience, but she herself does not think so. Answer (a) would imply that Agnes has more than enough money already, in which case there would be no need for her to leave the family to work elsewhere. Therefore we are left with option (b) Carefulness and good sense, as the only prudent answer!

Q11. How old is the narrator, Agnes?

a) **Under eighteen**
b) **Older than eighteen**
c) **Still a young child**
d) **In her late thirties**

Answer: B

A pure retrieval question, simply answered by examining line 32 where Agnes pleads "But mamma, I am above eighteen". Thus we have eliminated (a) and (c) as being impossible.

Answer d) In her late thirties is obviously "above eighteen", but remarks such as Agnes' mother's "...you have not learned to take care of *yourself* yet" in line 30 would hardly be addressed to somebody of that age. So (b) is the correct answer here.

Q12. Do you think that Agnes is an obedient daughter to her parents?

a) **Sometimes**
b) **Never**
c) **When it suits her**
d) **Always**

Answer: D

There is no absolutely direct quote to establish that Agnes is constantly an obedient daughter, but there are many hints in the text that she is indeed obedient to her parents. She immediately agrees to her mother's scheme for selling pictures. She is very keen on her plan to be a governess, yet after a mild attempt to justify her choice, she "was silenced for that day, and for many succeeding ones" (line 52) presumably to save her parents worry and abide by their wishes until she can persuade them differently. Finally, we can confirm that the best answer is **(d)** by examining Agnes' words in line 39: "You think, because *I always do as you bid me*, I have no judgement of my own..." Obviously this is Agnes' personal point of view, rather than a quote from her parents, but it rings true.

Q13. What type of word is "dejection"?

a) A noun
b) An adjective
c) An adverb
d) A proper noun

Answer: A

The correct answer is **(a)**. Dejection is a noun meaning a unhappy and defeated state of mind. The word does not describe another noun, so it cannot be an adjective. Nor does it describe a verb, and thus cannot be an adverb. So we may safely ignore options **(b)** and **(c)**. As for **(d)**, it must be discounted because a proper noun always takes a capital letter, and is usually the name of a person, place or organisation. There is no capital letter for dejection in the text.

Q14. How does Agnes' father react to her career plan?

a) He has mixed reactions
b) He thinks it an excellent idea
c) He is angry with her
d) He wants her to start immediately

Answer: A

This is a slightly more complex retrieval question, since Agnes' father is in a frail state of health, and his reaction to her plan to be a governess takes two forms within the extract.

Firstly, answers **(b)** and **(d)** can be eliminated, as nobody in the family reacts positively to Agnes' plan, and in line 48 her father says "Surely we are not brought to that pass yet." However, he does not seem at all angry, so option **(c)** can also be discarded. There is, however, evidence of both amusement (in lines 43-44) — "…he laughed at the idea" — and then sadness (line 47): "And a tear glistened in his eye as he added…". With this evidence, it is clear that answer a) is the correct one.

Q15. Does Mary believe her sister could be a governess?

  a) Yes, she is certain Agnes could do it easily
  b) No, she believes Agnes is too bad-tempered to be a governess
  c) No, she believes Agnes could not even choose appropriate clothes for the job
  d) Maybe – she wants Agnes to try it for a while and see what happens

Answer: C

Mary's reaction to her sister's announcement seems rather extreme, but her opinion can be found in lines 37-38: "...you would not even know what clothes to put on", implying that Agnes does not even know how to dress as a governess, let alone know how to do all the work required.

So the right answer is **(c)**. Answers **(a) (b)** and **(d)** have no support within the text.

Q16. What do you think Agnes' father means when he says "Afflicted as we are"?

  a) He means the whole family is unwell
  b) The Grey family is in a feud with another family
  c) The family is disliked by the local people
  d) The family has become very poor

Answer: D

An affliction is a cause of harm or pain, and there are several pointers as to how the family is "afflicted" in the extract as a whole.

Looking at the evidence throughout the text, we find nothing to support answer (**a**), because the three women in the household are fit and active, and ready to start work. There are no family feuds mentioned in the extract, so we may also reject answer (**b**). Although no family friends are specifically discussed, answer (**c**) has no textual support and is far less likely than (**d**): The family has become very poor.

The problem of lack of finances runs throughout the excerpt, exemplified by both family conversations and Agnes' own thoughts, as we see in line 5 — "But then you see there's no money" — and lines 56-57: "...To earn my own maintenance (living expenses), and something to comfort and help my father, mother and sister." So (**d**) is the outstandingly correct answer to this question.

Q17. What does the word "whim" in line 50 mean?

    a) **An annoying habit**
    b) **A selfish plan**
    c) **A sudden, odd idea**
    d) **An impertinent question**

Answer: C

At line 50, Agnes' mother dismisses her daughter's plan as "merely" a whim. Merely means only or simply, so we can infer that the word means something unimportant and trivial. We know that the family finds Agnes' "whim" amusing, even laughable, so answers (**a**) and (**b**) seem very unlikely.

Searching the extract shows that option (**d**) should be discounted, because Agnes has asked no question in the preceding paragraph, and given her character as portrayed here, we would not expect her to be impertinent; she always shows respect to her parents. Therefore we are left with the right definition of "whim": option (**c**) a sudden, odd idea.

Q18. What does Agnes do about her plan to be a governess after the family dismisses it?

a) She immediately drops all her plans
b) She decides to wait five years, then try again
c) She privately continues to think about her scheme
d) She ignores her family and applies for a job immediately

Answer: C

We have a more straightforward retrieval question again here. As we have seen, Agnes' family do dismiss her idea of being a governess as a "whim", but she herself, although appearing to agree to their opinion, says in lines 52-53: "I did not wholly relinquish (give up) my darling scheme." This is referenced again in line 54 when Agnes says "...while I drew I thought of other things..." and she continues her thoughts about her career plan, while saying nothing more to her relatives. Therefore the best answer here is (**c**).

Answers (**a**) and (**d**) have no support in this excerpt, and (**b**) can be discarded too, since the family's need to send the father away on holiday is immediate, and their financial problems could not sensibly wait five years to be solved.

Q 19. Why do you think Agnes describes herself as "little" when she says in line 43 "to show papa what his little Agnes could do"?

a) Because she is a very small woman
b) Because her father still thinks of her as a child, and she wants to prove him wrong
c) Because she thinks of herself as a little, helpless young woman who can't achieve much in life
d) Because she is shorter than her mother and sister

Answer: B

This question is perhaps a little trickier, but by examining the text carefully and using our elimination methods, we can pinpoint the best answer.

Firstly, there is no reference to Agnes' actual physical size in this passage. So answers (**a**) and (**d**) are unlikely and cannot be justified. Option (**c**) is worth considering, but as we see from lines 32-33 — "...I am above eighteen and quite able to take care of myself and others too. You do not know half the wisdom and prudence I possess..."

— Agnes does not see herself as her family see her, but as someone adult and competent.

The most likely answer is therefore (**b**), because Agnes seems to be calling herself "little" ironically, as an amusing contrast between her father's perception of her, and her own self-belief. She seems to feel her father is thinking of her as far more "little" than she really is, and seeing her as childishly incapable, which is a misapprehension she wishes to correct by proving her mature abilities to him.

Q20. How many family members do you think live in Agnes' house?

a) Five
b) Two
c) Four
d) Three

Answer: C

This question appears simple, although there is no statement of a particular number of family members in the text. We know there are at least four relatives in the house, as they all take part in this extract. We have Agnes the narrator, her mother, her sister Mary and her father who is unwell. So there cannot be fewer than this total, making options (**b**) and (**d**) clearly incorrect.

Now we need to check evidence of any other family member living with Agnes, so we can dismiss answer (**a**) and confirm the most likely option, (**c**).

Were there another family member present in the house, we might expect them not only to be mentioned, but also included in the plan to make enough money to send the father away on holiday. As Agnes is over eighteen, and is thought of as the "little" one of the family, a younger sibling than her is unlikely to live with them. An older male or female member of the family would certainly be asked to contribute to the finances in some way. Putting this evidence together, the best answer is certainly (**c**).

Q21. What does Agnes mean when she says "Only try me" in line 40?

a) Let me have an attempt at it
b) Put me on trial
c) Annoy me and see what happens

d) Try to ignore me

Answer: A

Option **(a)** is the right answer here, confirmed when Agnes repeats the expression in line 56 when she wants "to try my unknown powers". If we need to make sure that we can reject the other answers, we should observe that there is no question of a court trial, real or imagined, so option **(b)** has no relevance.

Option **(c)** is not something Agnes as portrayed here would say to her respected parents, and answer **(d)** cannot be right either, since Agnes has bravely put her plan forward, so would not wish to be ignored.

Q22. From line 55 (...to go out into the world...) to line 60 (...the helpless, thoughtless being they supposed.) there are seven examples of the same punctuation mark. What is it called?

   a) A full stop
   b) A comma
   c) An exclamation mark
   d) A semicolon

Answer: D

Here we have a punctuation question, and the correct answer is **(d)** a semicolon.

Semicolons link separate ideas or clauses (that are closely related) within one sentence, while separating them more clearly than a comma (answer b) would do. If read aloud, a semicolon would need a little more of a pause in a sentence than a comma would merit. Full stops **(a)** only come at the close of sentences, as do exclamation marks **(c)**, which are used to give a strong emphasis to what has been written.

Q23. Does Agnes remember how she felt as a child?

   a) Not at all
   b) Vaguely
   c) Clearly

d) **Occasionally**

Answer: C

A retrieval question again, which is best answered by checking lines 62-63 where Agnes herself says "The clear remembrance of my own thoughts and feelings in early childhood would be a surer guide..." There is no textual support for options **(a)**, **(b)** or **(d)**, so the right answer is c).

Q24. What do you think "to embolden the timid" in line 66 means?

    a) **To make shy ones braver**
    b) **To wake up sleepy ones**
    c) **To make lazy ones work harder**
    d) **To frighten the disobedient ones**

Answer: A

The final vocabulary question of the paper asks us what a particular phrase means, rather than wanting us to define just one word.

"Embolden" means to give courage, to make bold, or brave.

"Timid" means nervous, fearful or shy.

Therefore, our correct answer is **(a)**: to make shy ones braver

Q25. How do you think Agnes' family feel about her in general?

    1. **They do not feel very strongly about her**
    2. **They hope she will get work and leave home**
    3. **They feel she is a financial burden on them**
    4. **They are loving and protective of her**

Answer: D

Here we have a more general question to round up the paper and show that we have read and understood the extract as a whole. If there is time, it is worth finding references to eliminate the wrong options and isolate the best answer.

Firstly, let us look at answer **(a)**, which posits that Agnes' family do not feel very strongly about her. We can read at line 51 her mother's words: "You know very well we cannot part with *you*." This is just one of a number of remarks by Agnes' parents that lets us reject this option.

Similarly, answer **(b)** must be ignored, as we know Agnes' father has "a tear [glistening] in his eye" at the very thought of her leaving home. As for option **(c)**, this is never stated; in fact the opening words to this extract are "Through all our troubles, I never but once heard my mother complain of our want of money", and certainly no particular blame attaches to Agnes.

So we are left with our final option, for which there is plenty of support throughout the text. Perhaps Agnes feels her family are even <u>too</u> protective of her! In her father's words at the thought of Agnes going away: "...my darling, we could not spare you." Certainly **(d)** is the correct answer to this last question of the paper.

Paper Two: The Young Fur Traders
SCATTERSHOT PAPER; DEVILISH; 40 MINUTES

This extract is from an adventure novel published in 1856 and set in a fort settlement in the American Old West. At this point in the narrative, fifteen-year-old Charley Kennedy has had a bad fall from a horse.

1   Shortly after the catastrophe just related, Charley opened his eyes to consciousness, and aroused himself out of a prolonged fainting fit, under the combined influence of a strong constitution and the medical treatment of his friends.

In Red River there is only one *genuine* doctor; and as the settlement is fully sixty miles
5   long, he has enough to do, and is not always to be found when wanted, so that Charley had to rest content with amateur treatment in the meantime. Peter Mactavish was the first to try his powers. He was aware that laudanum had the effect of producing sleep, and seeing that Charley looked somewhat sleepy after recovering consciousness, he thought it advisable to help out that propensity to slumber, and
10   went to the medicine chest, whence he extracted a small phial of tincture of rhubarb, the half of which he emptied into a wineglass, under the impression that it was laudanum, and poured down Charley's throat! The poor boy swallowed a little, and sputtered the remainder over the bed-clothes. It may be remarked here that Mactavish was a wild, happy, half-mad sort of fellow—wonderfully erudite in regard
15   to some things, and profoundly ignorant in regard to others. Medicine, it need scarcely be added, was not his *forte*. Having accomplished this feat to his satisfaction, he sat down to watch by the bedside of his friend. Peter had taken this opportunity to

indulge in a little private practice just after several of the other gentlemen had left the office, under the impression that Charley had better remain quiet for a short time.

20 "Well, Peter," whispered Mr Kennedy, senior, putting his head in at the door (it was Harry's room in which Charley lay), "how is he now?"

"Oh! doing capitally," replied Peter, in a hoarse whisper, at the same time rising and entering the office, while he gently closed the door behind him. "I gave him a small dose of physic, which I think has done him good. He's sleeping like a top now."

25 "What did you give him?" Mr Kennedy inquired abruptly.

"Only a little laudanum."

"How much did you give him?" said the senior clerk, who had entered the apartment with Harry a few minutes before.

"Not quite a wineglassful," replied Peter, somewhat subdued.

30 "A what!" cried the father, starting from his chair as if he had received an electric shock, and rushing into the adjoining room, up and down which he raved in a state of distraction, being utterly ignorant of what should be done under the circumstances.

"Oh dear!" gasped Peter, turning pale as death.

35 Meanwhile the senior clerk had rushed to Tom Whyte.

"Go for the doctor, Tom, quick! run like the wind. Take the freshest horse; fly, Tom, Charley's poisoned—laudanum; quick!"

"'Eavens an' 'arth!" ejaculated the groom, wheeling round, and stalking rapidly off to the stable like a pair of insane compasses; while the senior clerk returned to the
40 bedroom, where he found Mr Kennedy still raving, Peter Mactavish still aghast and deadly pale, and Harry Somerville staring like a maniac at his young friend, as if he expected every moment to see him explode, although, to all appearance, he was sleeping soundly, and comfortably too, notwithstanding the noise that was going on around him. Suddenly Harry's eye rested on the label of the half-empty phial, and he
45 uttered a loud, prolonged cheer.

"It's only tincture of rhubarb," cried the boy, holding up the phial triumphantly.

"So it is, I declare," exclaimed Mr Kennedy, in a tone that indicated intense relief of mind; while Peter Mactavish uttered a sigh so deep that one might suppose a burden of innumerable tons weight had just been removed from his breast.

50 Charley had been roused from his slumbers by this last ebullition; but on being told what had caused it, he turned languidly round on his pillow and went to sleep again, while his friends departed and left him to repose.

Tom Whyte failed to find the doctor. The servant told him that her master had been suddenly called to set a broken leg that morning for a trapper who lived ten
55 miles *down* the river, and on his return had found a man waiting with a horse and cariole, who carried him violently away to see his wife, who had been taken suddenly ill at a house twenty miles *up* the river, and so she didn't expect him back that night.

"An' where has 'e been took to?" inquired Tom.

She couldn't tell; she knew it was somewhere about the White-horse Plains, but she
60 didn't know more than that.

"Did 'e not say w'en 'e'd be 'ome?"

"No, he didn't."

"Oh dear!" said Tom, rubbing his long nose in great perplexity. "It's an 'orrible case o' sudden and onexpected pison."

65 She was sorry for it, but couldn't help that; and thereupon, bidding him good-morning, shut the door.

An extract from The Young Fur Traders by R. M. Ballantyne

Q1. Two things influenced Charley to regain consciousness. One was his strong constitution (his basic good health). What was the other?

  a) A loud noise
  b) Some strong pills
  c) His friends' medical treatment
  d) His father's voice

Answer: ___

Q2. How long is the Red River settlement?

  a) Sixty miles long
  b) Fifty miles long
  c) Sixty yards long
  d) Sixty kilometres long

Answer: ___

Q3. Why did Charley have to "rest content with amateur treatment"?

a) Red River had no doctors at all
b) The doctors in Red River were away at a conference
c) Charley's father did not trust doctors
d) There was only one doctor in Red River

Answer: ___

Q4. What does the word "catastrophe" in line 1 mean?

a) A car crash
b) A joyful event
c) A disaster
d) A birthday

Answer: ___

Q5. The verb "sputtered" is an example of what figure of speech?

a) Personification
b) Onomatopoeia
c) Understatement
d) Exaggeration

Answer: ___

Q6. Why did Peter Mactavish give Charley what he thought was laudanum? (laudanum was a strong painkiller and sleep medication, of which the usual dose was only a few drops)

a) Peter was a doctor and was sure the medicine would wake Charley up
b) Peter disliked Charley and wanted to make him feel worse
c) Peter thought Charley had swallowed poison, and that laudanum was the antidote
d) Peter saw Charley was sleepy and wanted to help him sleep better

Answer: ___

Q7. Which word here has the nearest meaning to "erudite"?

a) Rude
b) Full of errors
c) Knowledgeable

d) Stupid

Answer: ___

Q8. Why was nobody but Peter watching Charley after his fall?

a) The others had left the room so Charley could have peace and quiet
b) There was nobody else at the fort that day
c) Only Peter knew Charley had fallen from a horse and hurt himself
d) The others didn't care what happened to Charley, so they left

Answer: ___

Q9. The name Red River is an example of:

a) Exclamation
b) Alliteration
c) Pun
d) Metaphor

Answer: ___

Q10. How did Charleys' father react when he thought his son had been given an overdose of laudanum?

a) He was furious with Peter and shouted at him
b) He thought it was a funny joke and started laughing
c) He refused to believe it and thought Peter was making it up
d) He was very shocked and didn't know what to do

Answer: ___

Q11. What type of words are these from the text: "capitally", "somewhere", "abruptly", "violently", "down"?

a) Verbs
b) Adjectives
c) Adverbs
d) Conjunctions

Answer: ___

Q12. "Physic" in line 24 is an old word for:

a) Poison
b) Physical exercise
c) Medicine
d) Physiotherapy

Answer: ___

Q13. What is the most accurate statement matching Peter's feelings when he found out he had not accidentally poisoned Charley?

a) He felt as if a heavy weight had been lifted from him
b) He felt annoyed that his plan to harm Charley had not worked
c) He didn't feel anything at all
d) He felt he had been unfairly blamed for harming Charley

Answer: ___

Q14. What do you understand by the phrase within the text: "Charley had been roused from his slumbers by this last ebullition"

a) Charley had fallen fast asleep after taking the medicine
b) Charley had been woken from sleep by Peter's sudden loud sigh
c) Charley had been woken from sleep by the sound of horses
d) Charley had been pulled out of bed by Peter

Answer: ___

Q15. Which word between line 50 (Charlie had been roused...) and line 57 (didn't expect them back that night") means in a slow, sleepy way?

a) Suddenly
b) Repose
c) Violently
d) Languidly

Answer: ___

Q16. Where was the trapper who needed his broken leg set?

a) Ten miles up the river

b) Ten miles down the river
c) Twenty miles up the river
d) Twenty miles down the river

Answer: ___

Q17. Which of these sentences contains a simile?

a) "Oh! Doing capitally" replied Peter in a hoarse whisper
b) "Not quite a wineglassful" replied Peter
c) "O dear!" gasped Peter, turning pale as death
d) "It's only tincture of rhubarb!" cried the boy

Answer: ___

Q18. The doctor was not at home. Where was he?

a) Somewhere about the White-horse Plains
b) Back at the Red River settlement
c) At his work surgery performing an operation
d) Nobody had any idea at all where he was

Answer: ___

Q19. "Medicine, it need scarcely be added, was not [Peter's] forte". Forte, pronounced either "fort" or "fortay", means somebody's:

a) Greatest skill or talent
b) Most hopeless failure
c) Lifelong career
d) Musical instrument

Answer: ___

Q20. The same punctuation mark occurs in the text after the words "doctor", "mind", "ebullition", "tell" and "that". What is it called?

a) A colon
b) An apostrophe
c) A hyphen
d) A semicolon

Q21. Why has the writer put the word "genuine" in line 4 in italics?

a) Because it is not an English word, but from another language
b) Because it is written sarcastically and means the opposite to what it says
c) Because italics give emphasis, and here stress the difference between professional doctors and helpful amateurs
d) Because the writer has taken a direct quote from another novel, and that has to be italicised

Answer: ___

Q22. The fort has a groom to look after the horses. What is his name?

a) Mr Kennedy
b) Peter Mactavish
c) Harry Somerville
d) Tom Whyte

Answer: ___

Q23. Harry stared at Charley as if he expected Charley to what?

a) Jump out of bed
b) Explode
c) Start screaming
d) Be sick

Answer: ___

Q24. Which of these clauses does <u>not</u> contain a pronoun?

a) "Charley opened his eyes to consciousness"
b) "I gave him a small dose of physic"
c) "Go for the doctor, Tom, quick!"
d) "She was sorry for it, but couldn't help that"

Answer: ___

Q25. Which of these options best sums up the last paragraphs of the extract?

a) Tom Whyte found the doctor and brought him straight back to the fort to look after Charley
b) Tom reached the doctor's house but the doctor refused to see him because he was busy with other cases
c) Tom reached the doctor's house and the servant told him the doctor could see Charley in a week's time
d) At the doctor's house, Tom spoke with his servant, who told Tom she did not know when the doctor would be back and then closed the door on him

Answer: ___

Paper Two: Answers & Guidance

Q1. Two things influenced Charley to regain consciousness. One was his strong constitution (his basic good health). What was the other?

  a) **A loud noise**
  b) **Some strong pills**
  c) **His friends' medical treatment**
  d) **His father's voice**

Answer: C

We're starting the paper with a fairly straightforward retrieval question which can be confirmed by examining the text at lines 2-3: "…aroused himself…under the combined influence of a strong constitution and the medical treatment of his friends." So the answer is (**c**).

As ever, if there is any doubt in your mind, it's a good idea to take a look at the other options. Here, (**a**) and (**d**) have no support at all in the text. Option (**b**) could be a possibility, since the whole passage is about a mistake made concerning medicine, but when the drug is given to Charley later it is meant to put him to sleep, rather than make him conscious. So we can reject (**b**) too, and feel happy with option (**c**).

. . .

Q2. How long is the Red River settlement?

a) Sixty miles long
b) Fifty miles long
c) Sixty yards long
d) Sixty kilometres long

Answer: A

The story is set in America in the 1800s, and America has never measured long distances in kilometres. They use miles, so answer (**d**) can be rejected. A yard is only three foot, less than a metre, so the Red River settlement could not be only sixty yards long – which excludes answer (**c**). Answers (**a**) and (**b**) both mention miles, so we can check the extract at lines 4-5 to find which is the correct one: "...and as the settlement is fully sixty miles long...". We see, then, that answer (**a**) is the one we want.

Q3. Why did Charley have to "rest content with amateur treatment"?

a) Red River had no doctors at all
b) The doctors in Red River were away at a conference
c) Charley's father did not trust doctors
d) There was only one doctor in Red River

Answer: D

An amateur is somebody who practises something - a sport, for instance – but who is not a qualified professional and does not get paid for it. The men at the fort settlement tried to help Charley, but, being amateurs and not actual doctors, were not sure what to do. To find the right option here, we can examine the text at lines 5-6. We are told that because of the large size of the settlement, the only doctor "...has enough to do, and is not always to be found when wanted, so that Charley had to rest content..." Thus the right answer is (**d**).

Q4. What does the word "catastrophe" in line 1 mean?

a) A car crash

b) **A joyful event**
c) **A disaster**
d) **A birthday**

Answer: C

A vocabulary question. If we don't recognise the word "catastrophe", we can look carefully at the context in which the word is used within the passage. We know from the description of where the extract comes in the novel, that Charley Kennedy has recently had an accident falling from a horse. This event, causing his unconsciousness, cannot be called "a joyful event" and no birthday is mentioned within the excerpt. So (**b**) and (**d**) are clearly wrong.

Answer (**a**) is certainly an accident, but there were no cars in Western America in the 1800s and we know it was a horse, not a vehicle, from which Charley fell. So the more general term "disaster", answer (**c**), is the one that matches "catastrophe". Other synonyms (words with the same meaning) are: "calamity" and "crisis".

Q5. The verb "sputtered" is an example of what figure of speech?

a) **Personification**
b) **Onomatopoeia**
c) **Understatement**
d) **Exaggeration**

Answer: B

"Sputtered" – like its near-homonyms (words that sound very similar) "spattered", "spluttered" and "splattered" – is an example of onomatopoeia, which is when a word echoes the noise it is describing. Therefore the right option here is (**b**).

Q6. Why did Peter Mactavish give Charley what he thought was laudanum? (laudanum was a strong painkiller and sleep medication, of which the usual dose was only a few drops)

a) **Peter was a doctor and was sure the medicine would wake Charley up**
   b) **Peter disliked Charley and wanted to make him feel worse**
   c) **Peter thought Charley had swallowed poison, and that laudanum was the antidote**
   d) **Peter saw Charley was sleepy and wanted to help him sleep better**

Answer: D

This is a slightly more complicated question. As we are told that Peter Mactavish was a "wild, happy, half-mad sort of fellow", it might be thought that he gave Charley the medicine out of sheer craziness. But if we examine the text we read that, seeing Charley looked sleepy, Peter wanted to "help out that propensity to slumber", in other words encourage Charley's tendency to sleep, by giving him laudanum, so that Charley got the rest he needed after his fall. This points to option (**d**).

We know Peter was not medically qualified, so (**a**) can be discarded. There is no suggestion in the text that Peter disliked Charley; in fact Peter was very worried about him as we see in lines 40-41 that Peter was "aghast (horrified) and deadly pale" when he thought he had poisoned the boy by mistake. So (**b**) has to be excluded as well.

Peter knew that Charley had fallen from a horse and not been poisoned prior to his unconsciousness, so (**c**) must go too, leaving us with the answer we originally understood from the text: option (**d**).

Q7. Which word here has the nearest meaning to "erudite"?

   a) **Rude**
   b) **Full of errors**
   c) **Knowledgeable**
   d) **Stupid**

Answer: C

Another vocabulary question, which can be answered by examining its context if the word is not recognised. The definition of "erudite" must be a positive one, since the context it is set in is putting up two opposing sides to Peter's character: profoundly (deeply) ignorant in regard to some matters, yet "erudite" in others. So the word must have an opposite meaning to ignorant. From the options available, only one is a positive adjective, and it is the correct one: **(c)** Knowledgeable.

Q8. Why was nobody but Peter watching Charley after his fall?

a) The others had left the room so Charley could have peace and quiet
b) There was nobody else at the fort that day
c) Only Peter knew Charley had fallen from a horse and hurt himself
d) The others didn't care what happened to Charley, so they left

Answer: A

A retrieval question which is answered in lines 18-19 where we learn that "…the other gentlemen had left the office, under the impression that Charley had better remain quiet for a short time." So the answer is **(a)**. The other options have no support within the text; we know there were others at the fort and they all knew about the accident. They certainly cared that Charley was hurt, considering one of them was his own father, and they had all been trying to awaken him after his faint.

Q9. The name Red River is an example of:

a) Exclamation
b) Alliteration
c) Pun
d) Metaphor

Answer: B

Both words in the settlement's name begin with the same letter, which makes the name an example of alliteration; answer **(b)**.

. . .

Q10. How did Charleys' father react when he thought his son had been given an overdose of laudanum?

   a) He was furious with Peter and shouted at him
   b) He thought it was a funny joke and started laughing
   c) He refused to believe it and thought Peter was making it up
   d) He was very shocked and didn't know what to do

Answer: D

Despite the possibly dangerous mistake Peter Mactavish made by giving Charley a large dose of medicine he believed to be laudanum, Charley's father did not shout at Peter and did not appear to blame him for the supposed disaster. Nor did Mr Kennedy think the event a funny joke – that would be an unlikely paternal reaction. He certainly did believe that Charley had been given the drug, as he started from his chair "as if he had received an electric shock" and then "raved in a state of distraction, being utterly ignorant of what should be done under the circumstances." This evidence leads us to the right answer: **(d)**.

Q11. What type of words are these from the text: "capitally", "somewhere", "abruptly", "violently", "down"?

   a) Verbs
   b) Adjectives
   c) Adverbs
   d) Conjunctions

Answer: C

The correct answer here is **(c)** because all the words are used in the text to describe verbs, so they are adverbs. Adverbs often do end in ly, but not always. There are many different kinds of adverbs, and "somewhere" is an adverb of place – other examples would include "above", "towards" and "behind". "Down" (as in "poured down Charley's throat" and "sat down to watch") is also an adverb of place in this extract.

. . .

Paper Two: Answers & Guidance 45

Q12. "Physic" in line 24 is an old word for:

   a) **Poison**
   b) **Physical exercise**
   c) **Medicine**
   d) **Physiotherapy**

Answer: C

The word "physic" has gone out of use, and is not used in modern medicine. To find the right option here, we must look at the evidence we can see in the source text. In lines 23-24, Peter says "I gave [Charley] a small dose of physic, which I think has done him good."

We know Peter believed he was simply helping Charley to sleep, so (**a**) can be rejected. You cannot give anyone, particularly someone in bed after a fall, a "dose" of either physical exercise or physiotherapy (the latter expression would be an anachronism – something out of its correct time – anyway), so (**b**) and (**d**) are not likely. (**c**), then, is the only right option here.

Q13. What is the most accurate statement matching Peter's feelings when he found out he had not accidentally poisoned Charley?

   a) **He felt as if a heavy weight had been lifted from him**
   b) **He felt annoyed that his plan to harm Charley had not worked**
   c) **He didn't feel anything at all**
   d) **He felt he had been unfairly blamed for harming Charley**

Answer: A

This point is addressed directly in the text at lines 48-49: "...one might suppose a burden of innumerable (too many to count) tons weight had just been removed from his breast." So we can see the correct answer is (**a**). The other answers have no support in the text.

Q14. What do you understand by the phrase within the text: "Charley had been roused from his slumbers by this last ebullition"

a) Charley had fallen fast asleep after taking the medicine
b) Charley had been woken from sleep by Peter's sudden loud sigh
c) Charley had been woken from sleep by the sound of horses
d) Charley had been pulled out of bed by Peter

Answer: B

This is a retrieval and a vocabulary question in one. The word "ebullition" is unusual and it means a sudden, loud expression of strong emotion. Following the text carefully, we can infer this meaning from the way that Charley reacts directly after we have been told that Peter "uttered a sigh so deep..." because of his relief at not having poisoned Charley. "Roused" means awakened, and "slumbers" means sleep, so the nearest explanation of the quotation in the question is answer (**b**).

To review the other answers if there is any doubt, we can be sure that no lullaby was sung, no sounds of horses are mentioned as waking Charley, and Peter, so relieved at Charley's not being poisoned, would not pull the boy out of bed. As a result, we can dismiss all other options but the right one.

Q15. Which word between line 50 (Charlie had been roused...) and line 57 (didn't expect them back that night") means in a slow, sleepy way?

a) Suddenly
b) Repose
c) Violently
d) Languidly

Answer: D

Another vocabulary test here, asking us to investigate a word within a specific passage in the text. We know that we are looking for a word that describes a verb – we are, after all, looking for a word that describes the way something was done – and thus we know are looking for an adverb. Since option (**b**) is a noun, it can be rejected.

Options (**a**) and (**c**) do not work, as they are both words describing agitated actions or feelings, and we know Charley is very tired and sleepy. If we look at line 51, we are told that "[Charley] turned languidly round on his pillow and went to sleep again...". Not only is "languidly" an adverb, it is also used just prior to Charley falling asleep again: a clue that it is associated with sleepy behaviour. Clearly, then, option (**d**) is correct.

Q16. Where was the trapper who needed his broken leg set?

    a) **Ten miles up the river**
    b) **Ten miles down the river**
    c) **Twenty miles up the river**
    d) **Twenty miles down the river**

Answer: B

These options might seem rather confusing at first. The doctor did have to go up *and* down river to see different patients, one ten miles away, and one twenty miles in the opposite direction. It is a good idea to check the text at lines 54-55 and find that the trapper with the broken leg was ten miles down the river from the doctor's house. So the right option is (**b**).

Q17. Which of these sentences contains a simile?

    a) **"Oh! Doing capitally" replied Peter in a hoarse whisper**
    b) **"Not quite a wineglassful" replied Peter**
    c) **"O dear!" gasped Peter, turning pale as death**
    d) **"It's only tincture of rhubarb!" cried the boy**

Answer: C

Here is a question about figures of speech. We are looking for a simile, which is a literary comparison of one thing to another using a conjunction such as "like" or "as" or "as if". There are no such comparisons in the answers (**a**), (**b**) or (**d**). However, answer (**c**) does contain the words "turning pale as death" which is a simile likening Peter's shocked white face to the paleness of a dead man. So (**c**) is correct.

Q18. The doctor was not at home. Where was he?

1. **Somewhere about the White-horse Plains**
2. **Back at the Red River settlement**
3. **At his work surgery performing an operation**
4. **Nobody had any idea at all where he was**

Answer: A

Here we have to find out where the doctor was, and we know he could not be at Red River, because if he was there to look after Charley, the groom would not have needed to go in search of him. So **(b)** is not an option here.

There is no mention of a doctor's surgery in the excerpt; the doctor *has* operated on a trapper's broken leg, but that was ten miles down river, and not at a surgery, so **(c)** is incorrect too. It is true that nobody at the fort settlement knew where the doctor was, but his servant did have some idea, so **(d)** is also excluded, which leaves us with **(a)**. At line 59 the servant "...knew it was somewhere about the White-horse Plains", so we can confirm **(a)** is right.

Q19. "Medicine, it need scarcely be added, was not [Peter's] forte". Forte, pronounced either "fort" or "fortay", means somebody's:

   a) **Greatest skill or talent**
   b) **Most hopeless failure**
   c) **Lifelong career**
   d) **Musical instrument**

Answer: A

The word "forte" is derived from the French word "fort" meaning strong, and refers to someone's speciality or the thing they are best at doing – their strength in life, in fact. The only definition that makes sense within the context is option **(a)**: greatest skill or talent.

Q20. The same punctuation mark occurs in the text after the words "doctor", "mind", "ebullition", "tell" and "that". What is it called?

a) A colon
b) An apostrophe
c) A hyphen
d) A semicolon

Answer: D

By examining the extract and finding the words mentioned in the question, we see that only one punctuation mark comes after all of these words. It is a semicolon, so the correct answer is (**d**). Remember that semicolons link separate but related clauses within a sentence.

Q21. Why has the writer put the word "genuine" in line 4 in italics?

a) Because it is not an English word, but from another language
b) Because it is written sarcastically and means the opposite to what it says
c) Because italics give emphasis, and here stress the difference between professional doctors and helpful amateurs
d) Because the writer has taken a direct quote from another novel, and that has to be italicised

Answer: C

Italics are used in text when special emphasis is wanted. However there are other reasons, including usage for titles of books, plays etc and sometimes for words from another language.

Answer (**a**) suggests this last use, but we can reject it because "genuine" is an English word. The writer is not using sarcasm (although there is an element of playfulness here, suggesting that there are many keen but ignorant amateur doctors in Red River) so (**b**) is incorrect; and the word is not a quote from another book, so (**d**) can also be discarded. The right answer is (**c**).

Q22. The fort has a groom to look after the horses. What is his name?

a) **Mr Kennedy**
b) **Peter Mactavish**
c) **Harry Somerville**
d) **Tom Whyte**

Answer: D

The options here are all the names of characters in the narrative, so we may want to do a quick check to find out who held the job of groom to the fort settlement.

Firstly, we know Charley's name is Charley Kennedy and Mr Kennedy is his father, often referred to as such in the text, so answer **(a)** is incorrect. Peter Mactavish - answer **(b)** - is the "wild, happy, half-mad" man who gives Charley the medicine, so he is not the groom either. Harry Somerville, named as Charley's "friend" does not enter the narrative until the groom has gone to fetch the doctor, so answer **(c)** also must be incorrect. At line 35 we read that the senior clerk of the fort "had rushed to Tom Whyte" and called on him to be quick and fetch the doctor. Tom Whyte replies: "'Eavens an' 'arth!" ejaculated (shouted) the groom, wheeling round and stalking rapidly off...". So the evidence shows that answer **(d)** is correct; the groom's name is Tom Whyte, the man who was sent to get the doctor for Charley.

Q23. Harry stared at Charley as if he expected Charley to what?

a) **Jump out of bed**
b) **Explode**
c) **Start screaming**
d) **Be sick**

Answer: B

A simpler retrieval question here, and we can find the answer directly described in the extract at lines 41-42: "...And Harry Somerville staring like a maniac at his young friend, as if he expected every moment to see him explode...". Thus the right answer is **(b)**. Just for fun, can you find a simile in the quote as well?

Q24. Which of these clauses does <u>not</u> contain a pronoun?

a) **"Charley opened his eyes to consciousness"**

b) "I gave him a small dose of physic"
c) "Go for the doctor, Tom, quick!"
d) "She was sorry for it, but couldn't help that"

Answer: C

This is one of those "odd one out" questions again, where we have to find something that is not there rather than something that is. Pronouns are used, as their name suggests, instead of endlessly repeating the same nouns again and again. So they help with both style and simplification of the narrative. There are different kinds of pronouns, and the ones we are dealing with here are personal pronouns such as "me", "you", "her", "them" etc and possessive pronouns like "my", "your", "their" etc.

In the first option we have "his" which is a possessive pronoun, so **(a)** is not correct. In the second option we can see "him", a personal pronoun, so **(b)** must be thrown out too. Option **(d)** contains the pronoun "she". So the correct option is **(c)**, which contains a common noun (the doctor) and a proper noun (Tom), but no pronouns at all.

Q25. Which of these options best sums up the last paragraphs of the extract?

a) Tom Whyte found the doctor and brought him straight back to the fort to look after Charley
b) Tom reached the doctor's house but the doctor refused to see him because he was busy with other cases
c) Tom reached the doctor's house and the servant told him the doctor could see Charley in a week's time
d) At the doctor's house, Tom spoke with his servant, who told Tom she did not know when the doctor would be back and then closed the door on him

Answer: D

The last question of this paper is testing our understanding of a certain part of the story, in this case the final paragraphs, from where we leave Charley and find out how

Tom got on searching for the doctor. Taking the answers one by one, let us make sure we have grasped the meaning of the end of the extract.

Answer **(a)** suggests that Tom had no problems, found the doctor and took him back to Red River. This is directly contradicted by line 57 where, after the servant has described why the doctor is away, she confirms that "...she didn't expect him back that night." Answer **(b)** has an element of truth, as the doctor has indeed had two other cases, but he is not there to refuse to see Charley, even if that were likely. Answer **(c)** has no support in the text, and if Charley had actually been poisoned, a visit from a doctor in a week's time would be useless. So we come to answer **(d)**, which is absolutely right and can be clearly confirmed by reading the last few lines of the extract.

The Three-Parter Paper

In contrast to the scattershot paper, the three-parter paper separates questions into different 'types': first, you have retrieval and inference questions; next, you have definition-style questions; and third, you have questions pertaining to language techniques.

It's important to note that just because a school has structured their paper one way in one year, this does not mean they will structure it the same the following year; however, there are a number of schools that separate their questions in ways similar to this, so it's definitely a style of paper to acclimatise to.

Notice that in both the papers that follow, each question has a choice of five options as opposed to four. It is important to note, however, that three-parter papers are not significantly more likely to have questions with five options as opposed to four – indeed, you can see five-option questions in other styles of paper too (including scattershot papers!).

You will also notice that the second three-parter paper in this guide revolves around a non-fiction piece as opposed to a fiction piece. Non-fiction pieces are rarer at 11+, but they do appear from time to time, so it is definitely useful to expend some effort familiarising ourselves with such extracts!

Paper Three: The Secret Garden
THREE-PARTER PAPER; DIFFICULT; 45 MINUTES

This extract is from a novel of 1911 by Frances Hodgson Burnett. In this extract, the orphan Mary Lennox has come from India and is travelling to Yorkshire to live with her uncle. She is accompanied by her uncle's housekeeper, Mrs Medlock.

---

1   She slept a long time, and when she awakened Mrs. Medlock had bought a lunchbasket at one of the stations and they had some chicken and cold beef and bread and butter and some hot tea. The rain seemed to be streaming down more heavily than ever and everybody in the station wore wet and glistening waterproofs.
5   The guard lighted the lamps in the carriage, and Mrs. Medlock cheered up very much over her tea and chicken and beef. She ate a great deal and afterward fell asleep herself, and Mary sat and stared at her and watched her fine bonnet slip on one side until she herself fell asleep once more in the corner of the carriage, lulled by the splashing of the rain against the windows. It was quite dark when she awakened
10 again. The train had stopped at a station and Mrs. Medlock was shaking her.

"You have had a sleep!" she said. "It's time to open your eyes! We're at Thwaite Station and we've got a long drive before us."

Mary stood up and tried to keep her eyes open while Mrs. Medlock collected her parcels. The little girl did not offer to help her, because in India native servants always
15 picked up or carried things and it seemed quite proper that other people should wait on one.

The station was a small one and nobody but themselves seemed to be getting out of the train. The station-master spoke to Mrs. Medlock in a rough, good-natured way, pronouncing his words in a queer broad fashion which Mary found out afterward was Yorkshire.

"I see tha's got back," he said. "An' tha's browt th' young 'un with thee."

"Aye, that's her," answered Mrs. Medlock, speaking with a Yorkshire accent herself and jerking her head over her shoulder toward Mary. "How's thy Missus?"

"Well enow. Th' carriage is waitin' outside for thee."

A brougham stood on the road before the little outside platform. Mary saw that it was a smart carriage and that it was a smart footman who helped her in. His long waterproof coat and the waterproof covering of his hat were shining and dripping with rain as everything was, the burly station-master included.

When he shut the door, mounted the box with the coachman, and they drove off, the little girl found herself seated in a comfortably cushioned corner, but she was not inclined to go to sleep again. She sat and looked out of the window, curious to see something of the road over which she was being driven to the queer place Mrs. Medlock had spoken of. She was not at all a timid child and she was not exactly frightened, but she felt that there was no knowing what might happen in a house with a hundred rooms nearly all shut up—a house standing on the edge of a moor.

"What is a moor?" she said suddenly to Mrs. Medlock.

"Look out of the window in about ten minutes and you'll see," the woman answered. "We've got to drive five miles across Missel Moor before we get to the Manor. You won't see much because it's a dark night, but you can see something."

Mary asked no more questions but waited in the darkness of her corner, keeping her eyes on the window. The carriage lamps cast rays of light a little distance ahead of them and she caught glimpses of the things they passed. After they had left the station they had driven through a tiny village and she had seen whitewashed cottages and the lights of a public house. Then they had passed a church and a vicarage and a little shop-window or so in a cottage with toys and sweets and odd things set out for sale. Then they were on the highroad and she saw hedges and trees. After that there seemed nothing different for a long time—or at least it seemed a long time to her.

At last the horses began to go more slowly, as if they were climbing up-hill, and presently there seemed to be no more hedges and no more trees. She could see nothing, in fact, but a dense darkness on either side. She leaned forward and pressed her face against the window just as the carriage gave a big jolt.

"Eh! We're on the moor now sure enough," said Mrs. Medlock.

The carriage lamps shed a yellow light on a rough-looking road which seemed to be cut through bushes and low growing things which ended in the great expanse of dark apparently spread out before and around them. A wind was rising and making a singular, wild, low, rushing sound.

"It's—it's not the sea, is it?" said Mary, looking round at her companion.

"No, not it," answered Mrs. Medlock. "Nor it isn't fields nor mountains, it's just miles and miles and miles of wild land that nothing grows on but heather and gorse and broom, and nothing lives on but wild ponies and sheep."

"I feel as if it might be the sea, if there were water on it," said Mary. "It sounds like the sea just now."

"That's the wind blowing through the bushes," Mrs. Medlock said. "It's a wild, dreary enough place to my mind, though there's plenty that likes it—particularly when the heather's in bloom."

On and on they drove through the darkness, and though the rain stopped, the wind rushed by and whistled and made strange sounds. The road went up and down, and several times the carriage passed over a little bridge beneath which water rushed very fast with a great deal of noise. Mary felt as if the drive would never come to an end and that the wide, bleak moor was a wide expanse of black ocean through which she was passing on a strip of dry land.

"I don't like it," she said to herself. "I don't like it," and she pinched her thin lips more tightly together.

An extract from The Secret Garden by Frances Hodgson Burnett

PART 1

Q1. Mrs Medlock cheered up because...

    a) She had slept for a long time
    b) It had stopped raining
    c) The guard had lit the lamps
    d) She ate a good lunch and drank tea
    e) The train had stopped at a station

Answer: ___

Q2. Where did Mrs Medlock and Mary get off the train?

a) The station where they bought the lunchbasket
b) At Thwaite station
c) At an unknown station
d) On Missel Moor
e) By the sea

Answer: ___

Q3. Mary did not help with the parcels because

a) She was too lazy and couldn't be bothered
b) She felt unwell
c) She was sleepy after the journey
d) She was used to having servants to do things for her
e) She was forbidden to help with them by Mrs Medlock

Answer: ___

Q4. Why was the footman's hat cover "shining"?

a) It was brand new
b) It was made of a glossy material
c) It was wet from the rain
d) The light of the moon shone directly on it
e) There was oil from the carriage wheels on it

Answer: ___

Q5. Mary did not go to sleep in the carriage because

a) She was curious to see the road they took
b) She had eaten too much to be able to sleep
c) She was too frightened of the journey to relax
d) She wanted to listen to the Yorkshire accents
e) The carriage was far too uncomfortable

Answer: ___

Q6. How many rooms did Mary believe were in the house where she was going?

a) Too many to count
b) Fifty
c) She had no idea how many there were
d) One hundred
e) Two hundred

Answer: ___

Q7. Why did Mrs Medlock say to Mary "You won't see much" of the moor?

a) The moor was covered in fog
b) The rain was too heavy
c) It was a dark night
d) The carriage window was dirty
e) The curtains were drawn

Answer: ___

Q8. Which of these buildings did Mary NOT see in the tiny village?

a) A public house
b) A church
c) A vicarage
d) A post office
e) A toy and sweet shop

Answer: ___

Q9. What did Mary do as "the carriage gave a big jolt"?

a) She settled against the comfortable cushions
b) She asked Mrs Medlock what a moor was
c) She saw the lights of the carriage lamps
d) She looked at the whitewashed cottages
e) She pressed her face against the window

Answer: ___

Q10. The horses began to go more slowly because...

a) There were more rocks on the road

b) The coachman had become sleepy
c) The rain meant the coachman could not see the road clearly
d) The carriage was going uphill
e) The horses were almost exhausted

Answer: ___

Q11. There was "a wild, low, rushing sound" because…

a) Mary and Mrs Medlock could hear the rough sea
b) The wind was rising and blowing through the bushes
c) The rain had turned into snow
d) The horses' hooves were going through mud
e) Other carriages were rushing past them

Answer: ___

Q12. How do you think Mrs Medlock feels about the moor?

a) She thinks it very beautiful
b) She only likes it when heather is blooming on it
c) She finds it bleak and savage
d) She thinks it too small and neat
e) She has no particular opinion about it

Answer: ___

Q13. What made "a great deal of noise" when the carriage passed over bridges?

a) The horses' hooves drumming on the rocky road
b) Mrs Medlock crying out suddenly
c) The horses whinnying because they disliked bridges
d) The coachman shouting at the horses
e) The rushing water under the bridge

Answer: ___

Q14. How did Mary feel about crossing the moor?

a) She did not like it and felt the journey was endless
b) She was not interested in the moor at all

c) She was scared and wouldn't look out the window
d) She was happy and excited to be on the moor
e) She slept through the journey and didn't notice it

Answer: ___

Q15. Considering the passage as a whole, the author presents Mary as:

a) A timid and nervous person
b) A loud, talkative person
c) An imaginative and curious person
d) A person who is not interested in anything
e) An extremely confident and optimistic person

Answer: ___

PART 2

Q16. What is the closest definition of the word "lulled"?

a) Annoyed
b) Awoken
c) Calmed
d) Bored
e) Interested

Answer: ___

Q17. What do you think "Thy missus" means?

a) The family
b) Your mother
c) The village
d) Your wife
e) Your daughters

Answer: ___

Q18. What is the closest definition of the word "burly"?

a) Slender
b) Healthy-looking
c) Plump
d) Tall
e) Heavily built

Answer: ___

Q19. What was a brougham?

a) A horse-drawn carriage
b) An early model of car
c) A broom made of twigs tied together
d) A Yorkshire borough
e) A steam train

Answer: ___

Q20. What is the closest definition of the word "bleak"?

a) Hideous
b) Desolate
c) Cold
d) Blessed
e) Grassy

Answer: ___

PART 3

Q21. Which of these words is an adjective?

a) Heavily
b) Wait
c) Fashion

d) Good-natured
e) Stopped

Answer: ___

Q22. Which of these words is a proper noun?

a) Bonnet
b) India
c) Native
d) Hundred
e) Coachman

Answer: ___

Q23. Which of these lines includes a metaphor?

a) "Mary stood up and tried to keep her eyes open"
b) "Look out of the window in about ten minutes"
c) After that there seemed nothing different for a long time"
d) "That's the wind blowing through the bushes"
e) "The wide, bleak moor was a wide expanse of black ocean"

Answer: ___

Q24. What types of words are these: "seemed"; "slip"; "is"; "pronouncing"; "said"; "pressed"?

a) Pronouns
b) Prepositions
c) Verbs
d) Adjectives
e) Conjunctions

Answer: ___

Q25. What word describes "tightly" in this quote: "She pinched her thin lips more tightly together"?

a) Adjective
b) Interjection

c) Verb
d) Noun
e) Adverb

Answer: ___

Paper Three: Answers & Guidance

PART 1

Q1. Mrs Medlock cheered up because…

    a) She had slept for a long time
    b) It had stopped raining
    c) The guard had lit the lamps
    d) She ate a good lunch and drank tea
    e) The train had stopped at a station

Answer: D

This first question is a retrieval question, where the answer can be found by looking carefully at the text and picking out the necessary word, phrase or sentence that answers the question most correctly.

At the beginning of the passage, we can see in lines 5-6 that the text reads "Mrs Medlock cheered up very much over her tea and chicken and beef. She ate a great deal…". Therefore the correct answer is **(d)**: she ate a good lunch and drank hot tea.

If we are unsure, it helps to eliminate anything that can be clearly shown to be wrong. Lines 3-4 — "The rain seemed to be streaming down more heavily" — helps us to reject answer **(b)** and the train doesn't stop until later in the paragraph, so **(e)** is wrong too. Mrs Medlock goes to sleep *after* cheering up over her meal, so **(a)** must go as well, and so must **(c)** as the lamps have been lit earlier at line 5.

If the answer, as here, can be gleaned easily from the text, and time is running out, it may not be necessary to find reasons to reject the wrong answers, but it is usually a good idea to make absolutely sure that no evidence has been missed.

Q2. Where did Mrs Medlock and Mary get off the train?

a) **The station where they bought the lunchbasket**
b) **At Thwaite station**
c) **At an unknown station**
d) **On Missel Moor**
e) **By the sea**

Answer: B

Another relatively clear retrieval question which involves examination of lines 11-12: "It's time to open your eyes! We're at Thwaite station..." – after which remark, the process of leaving the train begins. So answer **(b)** must be the right one.

The only other real possibility is answer **(a)** since the lunchbasket was bought at a station, but since Mary and Mrs Medlock ate at the beginning of the excerpt, that is not relevant. We know the station's name; the train does not reach the moor, and they never travel by the sea, so the answers **(c) (d)** and **(e)** must be incorrect, too.

Q3. Mary did not help with the parcels because

a) **She was too lazy and couldn't be bothered**
b) **She felt unwell**
c) **She was sleepy after the journey**
d) **She was used to having servants to do things for her**
e) **She was forbidden to help with them by Mrs Medlock**

Answer: D

Mary has come to Yorkshire from India, where she was accustomed to having servants who "always picked up or carried things" (lines 14-15) so **(d)** is the right answer here.

There is nothing in the passage to support answers **(a) (b)** or **(e)**. **(c)** could be a possibility, as we read that "Mary tried to keep her eyes open", but lines 14-15 are explicit about Mary's reason for not helping.

Q4. Why was the footman's hat cover "shining"?

    a) It was brand new
    b) It was made of a glossy material
    c) It was wet from the rain
    d) The light of the moon shone directly on it
    e) There was oil from the carriage wheels on it

Answer: C

There are two indications in the extract that **(c)** – it was wet from the rain – is the correct answer here. A hint in line 4 comes when we are told "everybody in the station wore wet and glistening waterproofs". "Glistening" is another word for the adjective "shining". Then when we meet the "smart" footman in line 26, we learn that "...the covering of his hat [was] shining and dripping with rain". There is no evidence to make us seriously consider the other options.

Q5. Mary did not go to sleep in the carriage because

    a) She was curious to see the road they took
    b) She had eaten too much to be able to sleep
    c) She was too frightened of the journey to relax
    d) She wanted to listen to the Yorkshire accents
    e) The carriage was far too uncomfortable

Answer: A

This is a slightly trickier question, because there is no obviously exact quotation from the text as to why Mary did not sleep in the carriage. Therefore we have to look for the most likely answer, by examining all the possibilities in turn.

Option **(b)** can be discounted because we read that Mary has already had a long sleep since her meal. Answer **(c)** cannot be right because in lines 33-34 we see that Mary "was not at all a timid child, and she was not exactly frightened..." Answer **(d)** does not make sense because Mary is alone inside the carriage with only Mrs Medlock, who keeps her Yorkshire accent to talk to local people (line 22). Then we can consider answer **(e)** but in line 30 we see that Mary is "seated in a comfortably cushioned corner" where she could presumably relax physically, so this answer must be eliminated too.

This leaves option **(a)**. As we read lines 31-23 — "She sat and looked out of the window, curious to see something of the road..." — we can deduce that this is the most likely answer of the five possibilities.

Q6. How many rooms did Mary believe were in the house where she was going?

    a) Too many to count
    b) Fifty
    c) She had no idea how many there were
    d) One hundred
    e) Two hundred

Answer: D

A more straightforward question here. Mary has the knowledge that the house she will be living in has a hundred rooms, as evidenced by lines 34-35 — "...what might happen in a house with a hundred rooms..." — so **(d)** is the only correct answer.

Q7. Why did Mrs Medlock say to Mary "You won't see much" of the moor?

    a) The moor was covered in fog
    b) The rain was too heavy
    c) It was a dark night
    d) The carriage window was dirty
    e) The curtains were drawn

Answer: C

An easily accessible answer again here, the answer to which can be lifted straight from lines 38-39 where Mrs Medlock says "You won't see much because it's a dark night…"

It is still raining at this point in the text, so **(b)** could be a possible answer, but the text is clear and there is no reason to be distracted from the right answer **(c)**.

Q8. Which of these buildings did Mary NOT see in the tiny village?

    a) **A public house**
    b) **A church**
    c) **A vicarage**
    d) **A post office**
    e) **A toy and sweet shop**

Answer: D

Here we have a slightly different sort of question, which asks us to find something that is absent, rather than look for information present within the text. From lines 42 to 47 several different types of building within a small village are listed, and the passage must be carefully checked to find the "odd one out" not described by the author.

Detailed examination of the appropriate passage will find a public house, a church, a vicarage and a toy and sweet shop, but no Post Office. Therefore the answer must be **(d)**.

Q9. What did Mary do as "the carriage gave a big jolt"?

    a) **She settled against the comfortable cushions**
    b) **She asked Mrs Medlock what a moor was**
    c) **She saw the lights of the carriage lamps**
    d) **She looked at the whitewashed cottages**
    e) **She pressed her face against the window**

Answer: E

A retrieval question, made slightly more difficult because Mary did actually do all of these things from **(a)** to **(e)** during the course of her journey. However, the exact reference we are looking for within the text comes at lines 50-51: "She leaned forward and pressed her face against the window just as the carriage gave a big jolt." So the answer is **(e)**. A jolt is a sudden bump or sharp knock; happening here as the carriage changes ground level when it goes onto the moor.

Q10. The horses began to go more slowly because…

    a) There were more rocks on the road
    b) The coachman had become sleepy
    c) The rain meant the coachman could not see the road clearly
    d) The carriage was going uphill
    e) The horses were almost exhausted

Answer: D

This is a "complete the sentence" style of question, hinging on the last word "because". If it is at all confusing, it can be reformulated into a "Why" question by changing its format thus: "*Why* did the horses begin to go more slowly?" so we can see, again, that it is a retrieval question needing a close reading of the appropriate part of the extract. At line 48 we find the relevant passage: "At last the horses began to go more slowly, as if they were climbing up-hill…" so the right answer is **(d)** and there is no textual evidence for the other answers.

It is important to look at and understand the context of a word or expression as it relates to the surrounding text, not to only see the isolated item. The conjunction "as if" here could be misunderstood to mean the horses are not really going uphill. However, "as if" is used because at this point in the text we are experiencing the journey through Mary's senses, and she is unable to see the horses ahead of her because she is inside the carriage and there is now a "dense darkness" outside. So we, like Mary, have to infer (use what evidence we *do* have to make up our minds) that the horses are going uphill, by feeling the slower movement of the carriage.

⋯

Q 11. There was "a wild, low, rushing sound" because...

a) Mary and Mrs Medlock could hear the rough sea
b) The wind was rising and blowing through the bushes
c) The rain had turned into snow
d) The horses' hooves were going through mud
e) Other carriages were rushing past them

Answer: B

Another "because" question; one that can be answered by reading the excerpt and finding not one, but two clear references to the rushing sound in the text. At lines 55-56 ("A wind was rising and making a singular, wild, low rushing sound") we see the exact quotation from the question. Then, if there was any doubt, at lines 61-62, when Mary has said she felt the sound might be made by the sea, we have Mrs Medlock confirming "That's the wind blowing through the bushes...". Therefore we know that (**b**) is the correct answer here.

Q12. How do you think Mrs Medlock feels about the moor?

a) She thinks it very beautiful
b) She only likes it when heather is blooming on it
c) She finds it bleak and savage
d) She thinks it too small and neat
e) She has no particular opinion about it

Answer C

This question is a trickier one. The answer can again be retrieved from the text, but there is an element of "a question within a question" here, as to some extent vocabulary is being tested as well as retrieval skills. Thus it may be a good idea to use elimination first, to leave us with the most likely answer.

We can see that (**a**) is not an option, since Mrs Medlock says nothing very positive herself about the landscape of the moor. She does allow that "there's plenty as likes it – when the heather's in bloom", but that is not her own opinion, so (**b**) must be rejected too. Option (**d**) does not make sense, since she herself says the moor is "miles and miles and miles of wild land", and since she does give her opinions freely about the moor to Mary, (e) is also incorrect. So we are left with answer (c). In the text, at lines 63-64, Mrs Medlock describes the moor as "a wild, dreary enough place to my mind" and we can confirm the answer when we know that "bleak" from the question has the same meaning as "dreary" in the answer, and similarly "wild" is a synonym (a word with the same meaning) for "savage". So the answer (c) is the right one.

Q13. What made "a great deal of noise" when the carriage passed over bridges?

    a) The horses' hooves drumming on the rocky road
    b) Mrs Medlock crying out suddenly
    c) The horses whinnying because they disliked bridges
    d) The coachman shouting at the horses
    e) The rushing water under the bridge

Answer: E

A simpler question here, to which the answer may be found in lines 68-69: "Several times the carriage passed over a little bridge beneath which water rushed very fast with a great deal of noise." Again, there is nothing in the text to support the other answers, so we will go with (e).

Q14. How did Mary feel about crossing the moor?

    a) She did not like it and felt the journey was endless
    b) She was not interested in the moor at all
    c) She was scared and wouldn't look out the window
    d) She was happy and excited to be on the moor
    e) She slept through the journey and didn't notice it

Answer: A

The final lines (69 to 73) hold the answer to this question. "Mary felt as if the drive would never end..." and "I don't like it" she said to herself, "I don't like it..." So we can see the answer is option (**a**). It seems logical that a child brought up in the heat and light of India might find it quite challenging to be on a cold, dark, wet moor in Yorkshire!

Q15. Considering the passage as a whole, the author presents Mary as:

   a) A timid and nervous person
   b) A loud, talkative person
   c) An imaginative and curious person
   d) A person who is not interested in anything
   e) An extremely confident and optimistic person

Answer: C

Question 15 is a more general, "summing up" question to finish the first part of the paper, and no single reference from a particular line of the text can produce the ideal answer. We need to show we have a broader understanding of the extract and the characters within it, which can be inferred from the many different sources, or hints, given throughout the extract.

Firstly we can look at each question for elimination purposes.

Option (**a**) asks if Mary is presented as a timid and nervous person. This is directly contradicted in line 33 — "She was not at all a timid child" — so we can reject it straight away.

Option (**b**) asks if Mary is presented as a loud, talkative person. This is less obvious, perhaps, but there are clues in the fact that Mary speaks only rarely throughout the excerpt, and we are told at line 40 that after "suddenly" (as if breaking a long silence) asking "What is a moor?" ... "Mary asked no more questions, but waited in the darkness of her corner". This is not a loud person, so we can eliminate answer (**b**).

When Mary *does* speak, it is usually to ask questions, as in line 36 ("What is a moor?") and line 57 ("It's – it's not the sea, is it?"); so when answer (**d**) suggests Mary is someone who is not interested in anything, we can reject it immediately, as uninterested people seldom ask questions. As for (**e**), which suggests Mary is extremely confident and optimistic, we can see by lines 33-34 that she has misgivings and a certain reserve about her destination: "She was not exactly frightened, but she felt that there was no knowing what might happen", so answer (**e**) does not fit Mary either.

This leaves us with answer **(c)** which posits that Mary is an imaginative and curious child. Can we find evidence to support this theory? Examining the text, we find line 31-32: "She sat and looked out the window, curious to see something of the road". So we know she can be curious to see where she is going. Mary asks questions and has a thirst for knowledge, and so, along with her keen observation of "the tiny village" that the carriage passes, we can confirm her curiosity. Her imaginative side is proven in line 61 — "I feel as if it might be the sea, if there were water on it" — and also in lines 69-71: "Mary felt as if the drive would never come to an end, and that the wide, bleak moor was a wide expanse of black ocean through which she was passing on a strip of dry land". These thoughts would only come to someone with a vivid imagination, and taking the evidence altogether, it should now be clear that option **(c)** is the best out of the five options to describe the way the author presents her heroine Mary.

PART 2

Q16. What is the closest definition of the word "lulled"?

  a) Annoyed
  b) Awoken
  c) Calmed
  d) Bored
  e) Interested

Answer: C

The second section of this paper is dedicated exclusively to single word definitions. As ever, even if you think you know the definition, it is wise to re-read the context in which the word appears, if only to double check that your chosen answer fits!

Moreover, if you are unsure of the answer, it can be useful to swap the original word in with each of the various choices you've been given in order to see which one seems to fit best. This is not guaranteed to work, but it at least lets you make an educated guess.

"Lulled" means calmed or soothed into a relaxed state, so **(c)** is the right answer. Mary was lulled to sleep by the noise of the rain splashing against the window.

Q17. What do you think "Thy missus" means?

a) The family
b) Your mother
c) The village
d) Your wife
e) Your daughters

Answer: D

"Thy" is Yorkshire dialect, and Old English, for "your". "Missus" means, as it sounds, simply "Mrs", which is a modernisation of the old honorific (title) "Mistress" which was given to married women. Therefore **(d)** is correct.

Q18. What is the closest definition of the word "burly"?

a) Slender
b) Healthy-looking
c) Plump
d) Tall
e) Heavily built

Answer: E

"Burly" is an adjective describing a person who is big and strong all over, not simply tall, or plump. So **(e)** "heavily built" is the best answer here.

Q19. What was a brougham?

a) A horse-drawn carriage
b) An early model of car
c) A broom made of twigs tied together
d) A Yorkshire borough
e) A steam train

Answer: A

A difficult vocabulary question, as the word is no longer in common usage, but a thorough reading of the text should make clear even to those who have never read or heard the word before, that the brougham (pronounced broom) that Mary and Mrs Medlock travelled in was a horse-drawn carriage: answer **(a)**.

Q20. What is the closest definition of the word "bleak"?

1. **Hideous**
2. **Desolate**
3. **Cold**
4. **Blessed**
5. **Grassy**

Answer: B

We have already looked at the word "bleak" in an earlier question, so we know it can mean "dreary". A further word with the same meaning is "desolate"; therefore **(b)** is the right answer.

This last section of the three-parter paper deals with parts of speech and figures of speech.

Parts of speech is the general term for the different functions of particular words in a sentence, for example: nouns, verbs, prepositions etc.

Figures of speech, such as similes, personification, metaphors etc are ways used by writers to give words special meaning other than their usual straightforward usage, so that the text carries more interest and emphasis.

PART 3

Q21. Which of these words is an adjective?

a) Heavily
b) Wait
c) Fashion
d) Good-natured
e) Stopped

Answer: D

An adjective is a word that describes, or modifies, a noun. The only word here that fits this definition is (**d**), "good-natured", which appears at line 18, and which is used to describe the station-master's friendly way of speaking.

Beware of confusing adjectives with adverbs like answer (**a**). Adverbs only modify verbs and they often end in "ly" – but not always.

Q22. Which of these words is a proper noun?

a) Bonnet
b) India
c) Native
d) Hundred
e) Coachman

Answer: B

Proper nouns can often be spotted in a sentence because they always take a capital letter. In this test, however, all answers begin with a capital. So we have to remember that proper nouns are usually the names of people, places and organisations. Months of the year and days of the week are also proper nouns and take capitals, as do specific, celebratory times such as Christmas or Easter. The only proper noun amongst these answers is a place name: India. So the right option here is (**b**).

Q23. Which of these lines includes a metaphor?

a) "Mary stood up and tried to keep her eyes open"
b) "Look out of the window in about ten minutes"
c) After that there seemed nothing different for a long time"
d) "That's the wind blowing through the bushes"

e) **"The wide, bleak moor was a wide expanse of black ocean"**

Answer: E

Metaphors compare one thing to another in order to imaginatively illustrate and/or emphasise a certain aspect of a subject. A metaphor does not include the words "like" or "as" which a simile uses, but instead is more direct.

As an example: "The clouds were grey curtains in a white sky" is a metaphor, while "The clouds looked like grey curtains in a white sky" is a simile.

The only answer here that compares one thing to another with no qualification is **(e)** "The wide, bleak moor was a wide expanse of black ocean", so that is the correct one.

Q24. What types of words are these: "seemed"; "slip"; "is"; "pronouncing"; "said"; "pressed"?

    a) **Pronouns**
    b) **Prepositions**
    c) **Verbs**
    d) **Adjectives**
    e) **Conjunctions**

Answer: C

Verbs indicate some form of action performed, and all the words in the question are action words using either the present or past tense. So answer **(c)** is the right one here.

Q25. What word describes "tightly" in this quote: "She pinched her thin lips more tightly together"?

    a) **Adjective**
    b) **Interjection**
    c) **Verb**
    d) **Noun**

e) Adverb

Answer: E

We have already noted that adverbs often end in "ly", and "tightly" modifies the word "pinched". So we can see **(e)** must be the correct answer. A possible problem here might be not knowing what answer **(b)** – an interjection – means (it is a word or words inserted to express a sudden thought or feeling); but once the clear and correct answer has been spotted, we can discount the remainder.

Paper Four: Sea and Sardinia
THREE-PARTER PAPER; DEVILISH; 45 MINUTES

This excerpt is from a non-fiction compilation of diary entries made by the English writer D. H. Lawrence, during a journey round the Italian island of Sardinia in the nineteen-twenties.

1   The bus sets off again—minus the old peasant. We retrace our road. A woman is leading a bay pony past the church, striding with long strides, so that her maroon skirt swings like a fan, and hauling the halter rope. Apparently the geranium red costume is Sunday only, the week-day is this maroon, or puce, or madder-brown.

5   Quickly and easily the bus slips down the hill into the valley. Wild, narrow valleys, with trees, and brown-legged cork trees. Across the other side a black and white peasant is working alone on a tiny terrace of the hill-side, a small, solitary figure, for all the world like a magpie in the distance. These people like being alone—solitary—one sees a single creature so often isolated among the wilds. This is different from
10 Sicily and Italy, where the people simply cannot be alone. They *must* be in twos and threes.

But it is Sunday morning, and the worker is exceptional. Along the road we pass various pedestrians, men in their black sheepskins, boys in their soldiers' remains. They are trudging from one village to another, across the wild valleys. And there is a
15 sense of Sunday morning freedom, of roving, as in an English countryside. Only the one old peasant works alone: and a goatherd watching his long-haired, white goats.

Beautiful the goats are: and so swift. They fly like white shadows along the road from us, then dart down-hill. I see one standing on a bough of an oak-tree, right in the tree, an enormous white tree-creature complacently munching up aloft, then rearing on her hind legs, so lengthy, and putting her slim paws far away on an upper, forward branch.

Whenever we come to a village we stop and get down, and our little conductor disappears into the post-office for the post-bag. This last is usually a limp affair, containing about three letters. The people crowd round—and many of them in very ragged costume. They look poor, and not attractive: perhaps a bit degenerate. It would seem as if the Italian instinct to get into rapid touch with the world were the healthy instinct after all. For in these isolated villages, which have been since time began far from any life-centre, there is an almost sordid look on the faces of the people. We must remember that the motor-bus is a great innovation. It has been running for five weeks only. I wonder for how many months it will continue.

For I am sure it cannot pay. Our first-class tickets cost, I believe, about twenty-seven francs each. The second class costs about three-quarters the first. Some parts of the journey we were very few passengers. The distance covered is so great, the population so thin, that even granted the passion for getting out of their own villages, which possesses all people now, still the bus cannot earn much more than an average of two hundred to three hundred francs a day. Which, with two men's wages, and petrol at its enormous price, and the cost of wear-and-tear, cannot possibly pay.

I asked the driver. He did not tell me what his wages were: I did not ask him. But he said the company paid for the keep and lodging for himself and mate at the stopping-places. This being Sunday, fewer people were travelling: a statement hard to believe. Once he had carried fifty people all the way from Tonara to Nuoro. Once! But it was in vain he protested. Ah well, he said, the bus carried the post, and the government paid a subsidy of so many thousands of lire a year: a goodly number. Apparently then the government was the loser, as usual. And there are hundreds, if not thousands of these omnibuses running the lonely districts of Italy and Sicily—Sardinia had a network of systems. They are splendid—and they are perhaps an absolute necessity for a nervous restless population which simply cannot keep still, and which finds some relief in being whirled about even on the *autovie*, as the bus-system is called.

The autovie are run by private companies, only subsidised by the government.

On we rush, through the morning—and at length see a large village, high on the summit beyond, stony on the high upland. But it has a magical look, as these tiny summit-cities have from the distance. They recall to me always my childish visions of Jerusalem, high against the air, and seeming to sparkle, and built in sharp cubes.

An extract from The Sea and Sardinia by D. H. Lawrence.

PART 1

Q1. The woman who appears in the opening paragraph is wearing a maroon skirt. However, excluding this individual, what colour skirts do women in Sardinia generally wear on a Sunday?

a) Maroon
b) Madder-brown
c) White
d) Geranium red
e) Puce

Answer: ___

Q2. The "striding" woman leads a pony of what kind?

a) Chestnut
b) Bay
c) Grey
d) Piebald
e) Shetland

Answer: ___

Q3. In lines 6-7 the author uses the phrase "a black and white peasant". What do you think this means?

a) The peasant is striped black and white
b) There are two peasants, one in black and one in white
c) The writer is colour blind
d) The writer is referring to the terrace where the peasant is working.

e) The peasant wears clothes that are both black and white

Answer: ___

Q4. The writer uses "hyperbole" (literary exaggeration, not meant to be taken literally) in lines 10-11. In which places does he say "people simply cannot be alone"?

a) Sardinia and Sicily
b) Sicily and Italy
c) England and Sicily
d) Sardinia and England
e) Italy and Sardinia

Answer: ___

Q5. In lines 12 to 16 which of these does the writer *not* mention seeing as the bus goes along the road?

a) Men in black sheepskins
b) A donkey and cart
c) Boys in soldier's old clothing
d) A goatherd
e) Various pedestrians

Answer: ___

Q6. What phrase in lines 8 (these people...) to 16 (white goats) describes the sense the writer feels when seeing the people walking from village to village?

a) A sense of being solitary
b) A sense of togetherness
c) A sense of Sunday morning freedom
d) A sense of disappointment
e) A sense of homesickness for England

Answer: ___

Q7. What does the writer think about the goats he sees?

a) He thinks they are beautiful

b) He thinks they are ugly
c) He thinks they smell
d) He is not interested in them
e) He dislikes all animals

Answer: ___

Q8. The phrase "a limp affair" in line 23 suggests that:

a) The post bag is full of letters and parcels
b) There is too much post and the bag is overflowing
c) The postman has a bad limp
d) The post bag is flat because there are few letters
e) The post bag is poorly made of cheap materials

Answer: ___

Q9. What does "The motor-bus is a great innovation" mean in line 29?

a) The bus has been successful for years
b) The bus service has been unpopular for years.
c) The bus service is completely new to the area
d) The local people cannot live their lives without the bus service
e) The bus is too big for local roads

Answer: ___

Q10. What is the average amount the writer thinks a bus can earn in a day?

a) Twenty-seven francs
b) Three quarters of twenty-seven francs
c) Three hundred to four hundred francs
d) Two hundred to three hundred francs
e) Two hundred to three hundred pounds

Answer: ___

Q11. What do you think the author means by the expression "The cost of wear and tear" in line 37?

a) The price of clothes and shoes

b) The cost of repairing everyday damage to the bus
c) The cost of paying the bus driver's wages
d) The cost of paying for fuel for the bus
e) The cost of expensive bus tickets

Answer: ___

Q12. The bus driver claimed he had once carried how many passengers to Nuoro?

a) A hundred passengers
b) Two passengers
c) Twenty passengers
d) Eighty passengers
e) Fifty passengers

Answer: ___

Q13. What is the local bus system called?

a) The Autovia
b) The Tonara
c) The Sardinian Bus Company
d) The Nuoro system
e) The Italian Transport system

Answer: ___

Q14. In line 53 what does the author mean by "summit-cities"?

a) Cities where international meetings are held
b) Cities that are built on stony ground
c) Cities famous for their mathematicians
d) Italian cities by the sea
e) Cities that are built high up on a hill

Answer: ___

Q15. Considering the passage as a whole, the writer presents the people of Sardinia as:

a) A nation of keen letter-writers

b) Sociable and very wealthy
c) Attractive and fashionably dressed
d) Solitary by nature but fond of travelling locally
e) People who rarely go out and prefer to stay at home

Answer: ___

PART 2

Q16. What is the closest definition of the word "peasant"?

a) A goat herd
b) Pleasant
c) A pheasant
d) A land-worker
e) A bus driver

Answer: ___

Q17. What is the closest definition of the word "complacently" in line 19?

a) Unconcernedly
b) Dangerously
c) Athletically
d) Comparatively
e) Cleverly

Answer: ___

Q18. What is the closest definition of the word "instinct"?

a) Insult
b) Natural feeling
c) Unnatural feeling
d) Stink
e) Necessity

Answer: ___

Q19. What is the closest definition to the word "subsidy"?

a) Subsequence
b) Government funding
c) Sunday service
d) Postage price
e) Substandard

Answer: ___

Q20. What is the closest definition to the word "isolated"?

a) Poverty-stricken
b) Insulated
c) Innocent
d) Lonely
e) Icelandic

Answer: ___

PART 3

Q21. Which of these clauses contains a simile?

a) "Where the people simply cannot be alone"
b) "This last is usually a limp affair"
c) "Her maroon skirt swings like a fan"
d) "I wonder for how many months it will continue"
e) "The distance covered is so great"

Answer: ___

Q22. What types of words are these: "puce"; "solitary"; "lengthy"; "splendid"; "private"?

a) Adjectives

b) Adverbs
c) Nouns
d) Pronouns
e) Prepositions

Answer: ___

Q23. Of what figure of speech is "brown-legged cork trees" an example?

a) Hyperbole
b) Simile
c) Understatement
d) Onomatopoeia
e) Personification

Answer: ___

Q24. Which of these words from the extract is an adverb?

a) Slim
b) Fewer
c) Goodly
d) Easily
e) Sparkle

Answer: ___

Q25. Which of these examples is an alliteration?

a) Narrow valleys
b) Madder-brown
c) Ragged costume
d) Private companies
e) Tiny terrace

Answer: ___

Paper Four: Answers & Guidance

PART 1

Q1. The woman who appears in the opening paragraph is wearing a maroon skirt. However, excluding this individual, what colour skirts do women in Sardinia generally wear on a Sunday?

   a) Burgundy
   b) Madder-brown
   c) White
   d) Geranium red
   e) Puce

Answer: D

All the answers here apart from **(c)** White, which is not mentioned in the paragraph, are variations on red. Burgundy is a dark brownish red; puce is reddish-pink and madder-brown is a reddish brown; but geranium-red is a strong scarlet, and that is the colour that the writer tells us is "Sunday only". So we see **(d)** is the correct answer.

. . .

Q2. The "striding" woman leads a pony of what kind?

a) Chestnut
b) Bay
c) Grey
d) Piebald
e) Shetland

Answer: B

These answers are all different colours of ponies' coats. Checking line 2 shows that the pony is described as "bay" so answer (**b**) is correct. Answer (**e**) Piebald is a more uncommon word and means the animal has white markings on a dark background, but this need not cause confusion as the right answer is clearly written in the text.

Q3. In lines 6-7 the author uses the phrase "a black and white peasant". What do you think this means?

a) The peasant is striped black and white
b) There are two peasants, one in black and one in white
c) The writer is colour blind
d) The writer is referring to the terrace where the peasant is working.
e) The peasant wears clothes that are both black and white

Answer: E

This is a less straightforward question after the previous simple retrieval ones. It is more a matter of deducing the writer's meaning in a way that makes sense. The writer of this extract has a personal style which is full of colour references and imaginative turns of phrase, so it is important that the text is read fully and carefully to the end before starting to answer the questions, so we can be "in tune" with his style and how he uses figures of speech.

Here we have the image of a "black and white" peasant working on a hillside, who the writer spots from his bus seat. He is far away and the author sees him as "small" and uses a simile to liken his figure to a magpie – a common black and white bird. So we can believe the writer just sees in the distance the black and the white clothes the peasant wears.

Obviously people are not striped, so let us discard answer (**a**). Only one "solitary" figure is mentioned, so (**b**) is wrong. There is no suggestion that the writer is colour-blind; in fact he has just written about the different shades of red in women's skirts, so (**c**) must be rejected too.

As the writer specifically calls the *peasant* black and white, not the terrace (bearing in mind also that this sort of "terrace" is part of a series of flattened agricultural areas on a hillside, so it would be green or earth coloured), answer (**d**) is not right either. So we are left with (**e**), which is certainly the best option, as a peasant's working clothes of white shirt and black trousers seems to fit best what the writer describes.

Q4. The writer uses "hyperbole" (literary exaggeration, not meant to be taken literally) in lines 10-11. In which places does he say "people simply cannot be alone"?

    a) Sardinia and Sicily
    b) Sicily and Italy
    c) England and Sicily
    d) Sardinia and England
    e) Italy and Sardinia

Answer: B

A retrieval question to deal with, which could be a little confusing because there are two places mentioned, but a check of the lines in question will show that (**b**) is the correct option.

The writer's use of hyperbole (meaning literary exaggeration) is interesting here. He describes people who "*Must* be in twos or threes" and "simply cannot be alone". No reader would believe that Italians and Sicilians cannot leave the house by themselves – the exaggeration is to emphasise his point and it typifies his colourful style.

Q5. In lines 12 to 16 which of these does the writer *not* mention seeing as the bus goes along the road?

    a) Men in black sheepskins

b) A donkey and cart
   c) Boys in soldier's old clothing
   d) A goatherd
   e) Various pedestrians

Answer: B

A different kind of question – the "odd one out" kind, which calls for a detailed look at the passage referenced.

(**a**), (**c**), (**d**) and (**e**) are all present in the extract, but there is no sign of a donkey and cart. Therefore (**b**) must be the option required.

Q6. What phrase in lines 8 (these people...) to 16 (white goats) describes the sense the writer feels when seeing the people walking from village to village?

   a) A sense of being solitary
   b) A sense of togetherness
   c) A sense of Sunday morning freedom
   d) A sense of disappointment
   e) A sense of homesickness for England

Answer: C

When Sunday was a religious day of rest from work for almost entire populations, it was the one time of the week workers had "freedom", and a Sunday morning walk was often habitual.

A check of the lines in question shows that (**c**) is the right answer.

Q7. What does the writer think about the goats he sees?

   a) He thinks they are beautiful
   b) He thinks they are ugly
   c) He thinks they smell
   d) He is not interested in them

e) He dislikes all animals

Answer: A

Scanning the paragraph the writer has used to describe the goats he sees from the bus, we see he uses positive adjectives and phrases to describe the goats: "swift"; "lengthy"; "slim"; "like white shadows". He uses the word "beautiful" at first. So it makes sense to reject all the answers except (**a**) as they are either negative or neutral.

Q8. The phrase "a limp affair" in line 23 suggests that:

a) The post bag is full of letters and parcels
b) There is too much post and the bag is overflowing
c) The postman has a bad limp
d) The post bag is flat because there are few letters
e) The post bag is poorly made of cheap materials

Answer: D

The word "affair" in this context simply means an object or an event. So one might go to see a boring film and call it "a dull affair", or look at a bad painting and call it "an ugly affair". The word "limp" when used as an adjective means weak and soft, so it describes something without much structure.

To answer this question, we can consider the options. (**a**) and (**b**) can be swiftly excluded, because we know the bag only contains "about three letters". We are told nothing about the postman's manner of walking, so (**d**) cannot be right, nor is the fabric of the bag itself discussed, so (**e**) must go too. This leaves (**d**) as the best answer.

Q9. What does "The motor-bus is a great innovation" mean in line 29?

a) The bus has been successful for years
b) The bus service has been unpopular for years.
c) The bus service is completely new to the area
d) The local people cannot live their lives without the bus service

e) **The bus is too big for local roads**

Answer: C

This is a question which in part relies on vocabulary, but also help can be retrieved from its surrounding text. If we do not immediately know the word innovation, and cannot infer it from its Latin root of nova: new; we can work out the meaning by examining the text for clues.

Directly after the quote in the question, the writer tells us the bus service in Sardinia "has been running for five weeks only". So this helps us to reject answers **(a)** and **(b)** since they talk in terms of years. Answer **(d)** must be considered very unlikely, as the local people have managed to live their lives quite happily without buses until five weeks before the writer visited Sardinia. Finally, there is absolutely no evidence in the text for **(e)** and we can see the journey has progressed without problems. We are left with option **(c)** which is the correct one, as an innovation is an occurrence of something new, and the adjective "great" emphasises the noun it precedes.

Q10. What is the average amount the writer thinks a bus can earn in a day?

   a) **Twenty-seven francs**
   b) **Three quarters of twenty-seven francs**
   c) **Three hundred to four hundred francs**
   d) **Two hundred to three hundred francs**
   e) **Two hundred to three hundred pounds**

Answer: D

A clearer retrieval question here, which only requires picking out the amount the writer estimates from the given text, although some of the options given are other figures within the text, so it's wise to check carefully.

The answer is **(d)** Two hundred to three hundred francs. This information can be found at lines 35-36.

. . .

Q11. What do you think the author means by the expression "The cost of wear and tear" in line 37?

   a) The price of clothes and shoes
   b) The cost of repairing everyday damage to the bus
   c) The cost of paying the bus driver's wages
   d) The cost of paying for fuel for the bus
   e) The cost of expensive bus tickets

Answer: B

"Wear and tear" is an expression which means the sort of damage that is caused to everything in life through habitual usage, even to our own bodies!

The writer is explaining his belief that the cost of paying for the upkeep of the buses to a certain standard, added to the other expenses the bus company have to pay, would make them eventually go out of business. So option (**b**) is the right one here.

Q12. The bus driver claimed he had once carried how many passengers to Nuoro?

   a) A hundred passengers
   b) Two passengers
   c) Twenty passengers
   d) Eighty passengers
   e) Fifty passengers

Answer: E

Again, a straightforward retrieval question, but we must be careful not to confuse the figures, if more than one is mentioned in the surrounding passage. So we can find the correct answer is (**e**).

Q13. What is the local bus system called?

   a) The Autovia

b) The Tonara
c) The Sardinian Bus Company
d) The Nuoro system
e) The Italian Transport system

Answer: A

All these answers are possibilities, in that none is outrageous or impossible, but the right option can be found by reading lines 48-49: "on the Autovie, as the bus system is called."

So (**a**) is correct.

Q14. In line 53 what does the author mean by "summit-cities"?

a. Cities where international meetings are held
b. Cities that are built on stony ground
c. Cities famous for their mathematicians
d. Italian cities by the sea
e. Cities that are built high up on a hill

Answer: E

International meetings of Heads of State can be called summits, but there is no indication in the text that the writer means that kind of summit. It is a comparatively new expression for a meeting, first coming into common use at the Geneva Summit in 1955, over thirty years after this journal was published. So we can discount answer (**a**).

We can also throw out (**c**) as completely unsupported by the text. (**d**) looks unlikely as we have no sight or sound of the sea within the extract. (**b**) is a slight possibility, since the "stony" ground is mentioned by the writer, but the overwhelming textual evidence: "High on the summit...on the high upland...high against the air" tells us that the best answer is (**e**). The writer's imaginative prose turns the distant village into a metaphorical city, because he is illustrating how, at a far distance and high up against the sky so that it is difficult to estimate the true size of it, the village can resemble a "magical...tiny summit-city".

. . .

Q15. Considering the passage as a whole, the writer presents the people of Sardinia as:

a) A nation of keen letter-writers
b) Sociable and very wealthy
c) Attractive and fashionably dressed
d) Solitary by nature but fond of travelling locally
e) People who rarely go out and prefer to stay at home

Answer: D

Here we have a "summing up" question to finish the first part of the paper. These more general questions cannot usually be answered by pulling out just one reference or quotation from the text, so it is sensible to go through the options and find evidence for or against them throughout the extract.

Firstly, if we take option (**a**), we remember the "limp" postbag in line 23 and the writer's estimate of it containing about three letters. So we can discount the idea of Sardinians being keen postal correspondents.

Option (**b**) – sociable and very wealthy – can be refuted in two parts. We have learnt that Sardinians are more solitary than other Italians (lines 6-7), which is the opposite of sociable. As for wealthy, the writer says "they look poor" and from the descriptions of the passers-by, the land-workers and the people at the post office, we can conclude it is not a very rich area.

Option (**c**) Attractive and well-dressed is similarly not likely, as the writer notes in line 24-25: "The people crowd around and many of them in very ragged costume" — and then, they are "not attractive: perhaps a bit degenerate". Degenerate means unattractive physically and morally, and is usually used of people who have come down to a low standard in life.

If we look at answer (**e**) we cannot find support for this; in fact in lines 12-13 the writer tells us "We pass various pedestrians" and there is a "sense of roving, as in an English countryside". So the Sardinian people like to be out and about and visiting others; in line 34 the writer notes the "passion for getting out of their own villages".

Finally we can approach answer (**d**), which is the remaining and right option.

This certainly seems the best answer to how the people of Sardinia are presented. The passion for travel just mentioned, plus the descriptions in lines 7-8 of their comparative need for solitude, tell us that we have chosen correctly.

Definitions of individual words as they appear in the passage.

PART 2

Q16. What is the closest definition of the word "peasant"?

    a) A goat herd
    b) Pleasant
    c) A pheasant
    d) A land-worker
    e) A bus driver

Answer: D

At line 7 we encounter the word "peasant" in the clause "Across the other side, a black and white peasant is working alone...". A peasant is an agricultural labourer or land-worker; therefore the option **(d)** is correct.

Q17. What is the closest definition of the word "complacently" in line 19?

    a) Unconcernedly
    b) Dangerously
    c) Athletically
    d) Comparatively
    e) Cleverly

Answer: A

In line 19 we see one of the white goats is in a tree, "complacently munching up aloft". The word "complacently" means in a self-satisfied or unconcerned manner, so the correct answer is **(a)**.

. . .

Q18. What is the closest definition of the word "instinct"?

a) Insult
b) Natural feeling
c) Unnatural feeling
d) Stink
e) Necessity

Answer: B

The noun "instinct" is used twice between lines 26 and 27: "It would seem as if the Italian instinct to get into rapid touch were the healthy instinct after all". We all have instincts, which in this case refer to natural and intuitive feelings and thoughts. So **(b)** is right here.

Q19. What is the closest definition to the word "subsidy"?

a) Subsequence
b) Government funding
c) Sunday service
d) Postage price
e) Substandard

Answer: B

In lines 42-43 the text clearly implies the meaning of this noun: "...the government paid a subsidy of so many thousands of lire a year..."; so even if the word has not been encountered before, it is clear that the answer is **(b)** Government funding.

Q20. What is the closest definition to the word "isolated"?

a) Poverty-stricken
b) Insulated
c) Innocent
d) Lonely
e) Icelandic

Answer: D

The meaning of this adjective can be inferred from examining lines 27-28: "for in these isolated villages, which have been since time began far from any life-centre...". So, isolated means remote; far from others; lonely; and thus **(d)** is the correct option.

PART 3

Q21. Which of these clauses contains a simile?

a) "Where the people simply cannot be alone"
b) "This last is usually a limp affair"
c) "Her maroon skirt swings like a fan"
d) "I wonder for how many months it will continue"
e) "The distance covered is so great"

Answer: C

A simile is a clause that compares one thing to another with the use of like; as; as if; or other similar constructions. Option **(c)** – her maroon skirt swings like a fan – compares the movement of the woman's skirt to the opening and closing of a hand-held fan, and is the right answer.

Q22. What types of words are these: "puce"; "solitary"; "lengthy"; "splendid"; "private"?

a) Adjectives
b) Adverbs
c) Nouns
d) Pronouns
e) Prepositions

Answer: A

All the words in the question are words which describe nouns, so the correct answer is (**a**), adjectives, because that is what adjectives do.

Q23. Of what figure of speech is "brown-legged cork trees" an example?

   a) **Hyperbole**
   b) **Simile**
   c) **Understatement**
   d) **Onomatopoeia**
   e) **Personification**

Answer: E

When a tree is described as having "brown legs" we know it must be a figure of speech, because a tree only has a trunk, not legs. However, people do have legs and personification is when a writer gives human characteristics to something other than a human. So the right answer is (**e**).

Q24. Which of these words from the extract is an adverb?

   a) **Slim**
   b) **Fewer**
   c) **Goodly**
   d) **Easily**
   e) **Sparkle**

Answer: D

An adverb qualifies or modifies a verb, so we are looking for a word that can describe an action here. Just to make it a little harder, there is a big red herring in the form of option (**c**): goodly. Often adverbs end in "ly", so an easy mistake to make would be assuming goodly is an adverb. In fact "goodly" is just an old-fashioned word for good, and is an adjective too. So we turn to the real answer which is the adverb "easily", option (**d**).

Q25. Which of these examples is an alliteration?

    a) Narrow valleys
    b) Madder-brown
    c) Ragged costume
    d) Private companies
    e) Tiny terrace

Answer: E

An alliteration is a phrase where the words begin with the same letter, usually two words in sequence; but it might be more words, or words divided by others, such as the phrase "The fair breeze blew, the white foam flew" from a poem by Coleridge. This last question of the paper contains one two-word alliteration: tiny terraces. So **(e)** is the right answer.

The Poetry Paper

The poetry paper stands out not because of how the questions are organised (indeed, they are usually organised in a way reminiscent of scattershot papers), but because the text the candidate needs to interact with is a poem instead of a piece of prose.

I would say that poetry comprehension papers are a good deal rarer than prose papers. That said, some schools do favour them. And, at the risk of sounding like a broken record, do keep in mind that schools are liable to change their style of paper from year to year – I have seen certain schools who have historically favoured prose comprehensions shift to poetry without warning – and we want to be prepared for all eventualities.

Generally speaking, poetry papers tend to have fewer questions in total than prose papers, if only because poems are usually shorter than prose pieces. This is nothing to stress about; it's just another quirk to be aware of.

Finally, a quick note about poetry itself. Many students find the thought of engaging with a poem intimidating. My advice is to keep a cool head, read through the text multiple times, and to accept that there might be words or phrases that the poet has intentionally made difficult – or even impossible – to fully understand. My other advice is to always be asking yourself: does the poet mean this literally or metaphorically?

Paper Five: On A Spaniel Called Beau

POETRY PAPER; DIFFICULT; 30 MINUTES

1   A spaniel, Beau, that fares like you,
Well fed, and at his ease,
Should wiser be than to pursue
Each trifle that he sees.

5   But you have kill'd a tiny bird,
Which flew not till to-day,
Against my orders, whom you heard
Forbidding you the prey.

Nor did you kill that you might eat,
10   And ease a doggish pain,
For him, though chased with furious heat,
You left where he was slain.

Nor was he of the thievish sort,
Or one whom blood allures,
15   But innocent was all his sport
Whom you have torn for yours.

My dog! what remedy remains,
Since, teach you all I can,
I see you, after all my pains,
20   So much resemble man!

William Cowper's 'On A Spaniel Called Beau'

Q1. Why is the poet angry with his dog?

a) Beau eats too much
b) Beau is a lazy dog
c) Beau has killed a mouse
d) Beau has killed a bird

Answer: ___

Q2. What does the word "fares" mean in line 1 of the poem?

a) Flies
b) Talks
c) Runs
d) Lives

Answer: ___

Q3. In this poem, the first and third lines rhyme, and so do the second and fourth lines, making the pattern ABAB CDCD EFEF etc. What is this rhyme scheme called?

a) Rhyming couplets
b) Alternate rhyme
c) Eye Rhymes
d) Half-rhymes

Answer: ___

Q4. The poet accuses his dog of a particular act in the third stanza. What is the nearest explanation of what the accusation is?

a) The poet accuses his dog of eating a mouse despite the dog not being hungry
b) The poet accuses his dog of not chasing the bird furiously enough
c) The poet accuses his dog of always being hungry and killing birds out of greed

d) The poet accuses his dog of killing the bird when he wasn't hungry, then leaving its uneaten body

Answer: ___

Q5. Which line from the poem contains an example of alliteration?

a) "Should wiser be, than to pursue"
b) "My dog! What remedy remains"
c) "And ease a doggish pain"
d) "Whom you have torn for yours"

Answer: ___

Q6. In the last stanza, there are seven punctuation marks. These consist of five commas and what else?

a) Two exclamation points
b) Two question marks
c) Three exclamation points
d) Two semicolons

Answer: ___

Q7. What two lines in the poem tell us that Beau had been warned to leave the bird alone?

a) "Nor was he of the thievish sort, Or one whom blood allures"
b) "But you have kill'd a tiny bird, which flew not till today"
c) "Against my orders, whom you heard forbidding you the prey"
d) "But innocent was all his sport, whom you have torn for yours"

Answer: ___

Q8. What do you think the poet means by "...one whom blood allures" in line 14?

a) A vampire bat
b) Someone who dislikes seeing blood
c) A warm-blooded prey animal
d) A predator attracted by blood

Answer: ___

Q9. What types of words are these in the poem: "thievish", "doggish", "furious", "tiny"?

   a) Adverbs
   b) Pronouns
   c) Adjectives
   d) Proper nouns

Answer: ___

Q10. The last verse in this poem gives it a surprising and humorous ending. What does it say about the poet's opinion of his own species as opposed to that of dogs?

a) The poet has a higher opinion of mankind than he has of dogs

b) The poet thinks mankind has a lot to teach dogs but dogs can teach mankind nothing

c) The poet has a low opinion of mankind and was hoping his dog would behave better than men do

d) The poet thinks dogs always behave better than man, whatever the circumstances

Answer: ___

Paper Five: Answers & Guidance

Q1. Why is the poet angry with his dog?

   a) Beau eats too much
   b) Beau is a lazy dog
   c) Beau has killed a mouse
   d) Beau has killed a bird

Answer: C

We have a straightforward question here about the reason the poet wrote this verse. The poem is a humorous one, as obviously Beau the spaniel cannot read or understand poetry, still less respond to the charges laid against him. However, the poet did in fact imagine his dog's answer to the poem, and wrote it in a poem called "Beau's Reply", which is amusing too, although both poems raise serious questions about moral behaviour.

Addressing the question, the right answer is **(c)** as we can read in the first two lines of the second stanza of the poem: "But you have kill'd a tiny bird, which flew not till today"

Q2. What does the word "fares" mean in line 1 of the poem?

a) Flies
b) Talks
c) Runs
d) Lives

Answer: D

"A spaniel, Beau, that fares like you," is the opening line of the poem. As it is describing the life of a dog, we must reject answers **(a)** and **(b)** because dogs can neither fly nor talk. They can certainly run, but "run" does not make sense here as the poet is referring to Beau's general condition: "well fed and at his ease", meaning he has enough to eat and does not have to work for a living. So the best answer is **(d)** here.

Q3. In this poem, the first and third lines rhyme, and so do the second and fourth lines, making the pattern ABAB CDCD EFEF etc. What is this rhyme scheme called?

a) Rhyming couplets
b) Alternate rhyme
c) Eye Rhymes
d) Half-rhymes

Answer: B

There are many forms of rhyme schemes, and of course some poems are written in blank verse, which means no rhymes at all. The options here are all worth considering so that we can isolate the correct one. Rhyming couplets are when the rhyme scheme is AA, BB, CC etc. Here is an example from "Sir Eglamour" by Samuel Rowlands:

"Sir Eglamour, that worthy knight,
He took his sword and went to fight:
And as he rode both hill and dale,
Armed upon his shirt of mail..."

However, we can see that rhyming couplets do *not* appear in the poem we are being questioned about, so we must reject answer (**a**).

Eye rhymes are when the final words of each line look as if they rhyme, but do not actually do so when read aloud, such as in "food" and "wood" or "cough" and "enough". So answer (**c**) does not match the poem either.

Half rhymes, or imperfect rhymes as they are sometimes called, only have the last consonant in common (although they do sometimes have more letters in common than that). An example of two words that, when combined, create a half rhyme would be "break" and "sack" – and another example would be "find" and "wand". This, again, is *not* the rhyme scheme we find in the poem above, so option (**d**) is incorrect.

We are therefore left with answer (**b**), alternate rhyme, which describes exactly what the poet has written in the poem above. Alternate rhyme means that every other line rhymes, in an ABAB form, so (**b**) is the correct option here.

Q4. The poet accuses his dog of a particular act in the third stanza. What is the nearest explanation of what the accusation is?

   a) **The poet accuses his dog of eating a mouse despite the dog not being hungry**
   b) **The poet accuses his dog of not chasing the bird furiously enough**
   c) **The poet accuses his dog of always being hungry and killing birds out of greed**
   d) **The poet accuses his dog of killing the bird when he wasn't hungry, then leaving its uneaten body**

Answer: D

Beau the spaniel has not killed a mouse, but a little bird, so we can immediately dismiss answer (**a**) here. The poet is annoyed with Beau for chasing the bird, so he would not want him to have chased it more furiously; this excludes answer (**b**) too.

Beau has already been described as "well fed" by the poet. Indeed, the poet explicitly points out that Beau did not kill out of greed or hunger – "Nor did you kill, that you might eat" – so we can also reject option (**c**).

What upsets the poet most is the waste of life, as Beau left the bird's body "where he was slain" and only killed the bird for fun, or "sport". So the last answer, (**d**), is the right one.

Q5. Which line from the poem contains an example of alliteration?

    a) "Should wiser be, than to pursue"
    b) "My dog! What remedy remains"
    c) "And ease a doggish pain"
    d) "Whom you have torn for yours"

Answer: B

Alliteration, as we have seen, is when two or more adjacent words begin with the same letter. So the correct answer to this question is (**b**) as the line contains the words "remedy remains".

Q6. In the last stanza, there are seven punctuation marks. These consist of five commas and what else?

    a) Two exclamation points
    b) Two question marks
    c) Three exclamation points
    d) Two semicolons

Answer: A

In this last stanza, the poet is making a partially humorous, but heartfelt cry to his dog, and to emphasise the strength of his feeling, he uses two exclamation points. So the right answer to this question is (**a**).

Q7. What two lines in the poem tell us that Beau had been warned to leave the bird alone?

    a) "Nor was he of the thievish sort, Or one whom blood allures"

b) "But you have kill'd a tiny bird, which flew not till today"
c) "Against my orders, whom you heard forbidding you the prey"
d) "But innocent was all his sport, whom you have torn for yours"

Answer: C

The poet says that he has already told Beau not to harm the fledgling. A fledgling is a bird who has only just learned to fly, and we know the bird was in this state, from line 6: "Which flew not till today". The line which tells us that Beau had been warned not to chase the vulnerable bird is at answer (**c**): "...whom you heard forbidding you the prey."

Q8. What do you think the poet means by "...one whom blood allures" in line 14?

    a) **A vampire bat**
    b) **Someone who dislikes seeing blood**
    c) **A warm-blooded prey animal**
    d) **A predator attracted by blood**

Answer: D

The poet is saying here that Beau has killed a bird which would never have killed anything else. Some birds, such as vultures, crows, and birds of prey (predators) in general, are attracted by blood – so *they* are those "whom blood allures". So the right answer here is (**d**). The poet is saying the bird Beau killed was *not* one of these types of birds, but he mentions them to imply that if it had been, that might have been a slight excuse for the dog's behaviour.

Q9. What types of words are these in the poem: "thievish", "doggish", "furious", "tiny"?

    a) **Adverbs**
    b) **Pronouns**
    c) **Adjectives**
    d) **Proper nouns**

Answer: C

All these words from the text are words used to describe nouns, so they are adjectives and the answer is (**c**).

Q10. The last verse in this poem gives it a surprising and humorous ending. What does it say about the poet's opinion of his own species as opposed to that of dogs?

   a) The poet has a higher opinion of mankind than he has of dogs
   b) The poet thinks mankind has a lot to teach dogs but dogs can teach mankind nothing
   c) The poet has a low opinion of mankind and was hoping his dog would behave better than men do
   d) The poet thinks dogs always behave better than man, whatever the circumstances

Answer: C

This poem is a humorous one, but in its final stanza the poet is making a serious point about his own species. He had hoped he had taught his dog to be different from mankind, who he implies is a species that cruelly kills for sport, rather than hunger or defence. Sadly for the poet, his dog does not live by the standards his master has tried to give him, but is more like the rest of the poet's race.

If we look at answers (**a**) and (**b**) we can see they are quite wrong, since the poet has a low opinion of his fellow men. Answer (**d**) has some merit, but cannot be right, because Beau has just behaved in a disappointing way that resembles human behaviour. So answer (**c**) is left, and we can see it explains the poet's views in the clearest way, and is the correct answer to this last question.

Paper Six: The Cat and the Moon
POETRY PAPER; DEVILISH; 30 MINUTES

1   The cat went here and there
       And the moon spun round like a top,
       And the nearest kin of the moon,
       The creeping cat, looked up.
5   Black Minnaloushe stared at the moon,
       For, wander and wail as he would,
       The pure cold light in the sky
       Troubled his animal blood.
       Minnaloushe runs in the grass
10   Lifting his delicate feet.
       Do you dance, Minnaloushe, do you dance?
       When two close kindred meet,
       What better than call a dance?
       Maybe the moon may learn,
15   Tired of that courtly fashion,
       A new dance turn.
       Minnaloushe creeps through the grass
       From moonlit place to place,
       The sacred moon overhead
20   Has taken a new phase.
       Does Minnaloushe know that his pupils
       Will pass from change to change,
       And that from round to crescent,

From crescent to round they range?
25 Minnaloushe creeps through the grass
Alone, important and wise,
And lifts to the changing moon
His changing eyes.

William Butler Yeats' The Cat and the Moon

Q1. Who is the narrator of this poem?

a) The cat Minnaloushe
b) Another cat
c) The poet/observer
d) The moon

Q2. In line 2, what do you think the poet means by writing "The moon spun round like a top"?

a) The moon suddenly fell forwards as if someone had pushed it
b) The moon jumped backwards in shock when it saw the cat
c) The poet is imagining himself spinning round by the light of the moon
d) The poet is looking at the moon from the fast-moving cat's point of view

Q3. What figure of speech is in line 4 of the poem?

a) Simile
b) Onomatopoeia
c) Alliteration
d) Personification

Q4. At line 9 in the poem, the poet changes from using one tense to another. Does he change:

a) From the past to the present tense
b) From the past to the future tense
c) From the present to the past tense
d) From the future to the present tense

Q5. What does the word "kin" mean in line 3?

a) Kitten
b) Close friend
c) Star
d) Family member

Q6. The narrator of the poem (the poet) suddenly stops watching the scene and asks a direct question. What is it?

a) He asks the moon if it dances
b) He asks the cat if it dances
c) He asks the moon if the cat dances
d) He asks the cat if the moon dances

Q7. In line 11, the word "dance" is used as a verb. What type of word is "dance" in line 13?

a) A pronoun
b) A noun
c) A verb
d) A conjunction

Q8. What is the meaning of the word "pupils" in line 21?

a) Schoolchildren in general
b) The eyelids
c) The whites of the eye
d) The black circles in the middle of the eye

Q9. The poet only uses three types of punctuation to end the lines in this poem. Which of these punctuation marks does he NOT use throughout the poem?

a) Question mark
b) Comma
c) Semicolon
d) Full stop

Q10. Why do you think the poet uses the word "changing" twice within the last two lines?

a) To finish the poem by emphasising the similarities between the moon and the cat

b) To simply make a repetitive noise when the poem is read aloud
c) The poet had run out of things to say so just used the same word
d) The poet made an error of literary style

Paper Six: Answers & Guidance

Q1. Who is the narrator of this poem?

    a) The cat Minnaloushe
    b) Another cat
    c) The poet/observer
    d) The moon

Answer: C

A first reading of the poem reveals that the action taking place between the cat and the moon is watched by an observer, a third person, in this case the poet himself. So the answer is **(c)**. Minnaloushe was in fact a real cat, owned by the woman loved by the poet W.B. Yeats, so we can imagine he did really watch the cat doing its moonlit "dance" and was inspired to write about it.

Q2. In line 2, what do you think the poet means by writing "The moon spun round like a top"?

    a) The moon suddenly fell forwards as if someone had pushed it
    b) The moon jumped backwards in shock when it saw the cat

c) **The poet is imagining himself spinning round by the light of the moon**
d) **The poet is looking at the moon from the fast-moving cat's point of view**

Answer: D

This is not a retrieval question, but one that requires interpretation, so we are looking for the most likely answer here. A top is a child's toy that spins fast on its own axis in a rotating motion. The poet is not suggesting the moon itself is jumping backwards or forwards, so we can reject answers **(a)** and **(b)** first. As we have established, the poet is also the narrator of the poem. He is describing the cat's behaviour in the garden, not his own behaviour – real or imagined – so **(c)** is far less likely than our final and most likely option: **(d)**.

The cat's eye is caught by the flashing of the moon's light as he dances "here and there", making the moon appear to spin in the sky as we see it sparkling from the moving cat's point of view.

Q3. What figure of speech is in line 4 of the poem?

a) **Simile**
b) **Onomatopoeia**
c) **Alliteration**
d) **Personification**

Answer: C

In line 4 we see the phrase "creeping cat". Alliteration is when a writer uses the same letter to begin two or more words which are next to or close to each other within a passage of writing. So **(c)** is the correct answer. Can you find another alliteration in line 6 ?

Q4. At line 9 in the poem, the poet changes from using one tense to another. Does he change:

a) **From the past to the present tense**
b) **From the past to the future tense**
c) **From the present to the past tense**
d) **From the future to the present tense**

Answer: A

If we take the verbs from the first 8 lines of the poem, we have: "went"; "spun"; "looked"; "stared" and "troubled". These are all verbs formed in the past tense, so we can dismiss answers **(c)** and **(d)** which put the first lines in the present tense and the future tense respectively.

From line 9 the verbs are different, including "runs"; "meet"; creeps"; "range"; "lifts". These are not in the future tense so **(b)** is also incorrect. The last twenty lines of the poem are in the present tense, making **(a)** the right answer here. It is worth noting, however, that there is *one* verb in the future tense at line 22: "will pass", and one verb in the present perfect tense at line 20: "has taken".

Q5. What does the word "kin" mean in line 3?

a) **Kitten**
b) **Close friend**
c) **Star**
d) **Family member**

Answer: D

The word "kin" comes from the Old English "cynn" meaning "family", so the right answer here is **(d)**. Quite a few of our words contain the prefix "kin", all relating to the family: kindred; kinship; kinfolk. If one thing resembles another, we say they are "akin" to each other.

Q6. The narrator of the poem (the poet) suddenly stops watching the scene and asks a direct question. What is it?

a) **He asks the moon if it dances**

b) He asks the cat if it dances
c) He asks the moon if the cat dances
d) He asks the cat if the moon dances

Answer: B

A clear retrieval question here, which can be answered by reading line 11 of the poem. The poet directly questions the cat: "Do you dance, Minnaloushe, do you dance?" So we can see that (b) is the right option.

Q7. In line 11, the word "dance" is used as a verb. What type of word is "dance" in line 13?

a) A pronoun
b) A noun
c) A verb
d) A conjunction

Answer: B

Many words can be used as a noun and a verb as well, without their spelling being changed. In line 13 the indefinite article "a" precedes (goes in front of) the word "dance" which indicates it has become a noun: *a* dance, instead of the word on its own as an action word. So the answer is (b). You can probably think of plenty of similar examples, such as: you run (verb) but you go for *a* run (noun), or you walk (verb), but you have *a* walk (noun).

Q8. What is the meaning of the word "pupils" in line 21?

a) Schoolchildren in general
b) The eyelids
c) The whites of the eye
d) The black circles in the middle of the eye

Answer: D

The word "pupils" can indeed mean people who are learning, but that definition does not make any sense in the context of this poem about a cat and the moon. So answer (**a**) can be rejected straight away as there are no schoolchildren mentioned.

The other answers all refer to parts of the eye, but there is only one part of the eye of cat or man that changes size all the time, and that is the black central circle, or pupil, of the eye. This means we can dismiss options (**b**) and (**c**) and focus on (**d**). In our own eyes we can test our pupils' reaction to light by observing how small the pupils become in bright light, compared to their larger size in gloom or darkness. The poet here uses the particular shape of a cat's pupil, which shrinks from round to more of a crescent shape in strong light, to illustrate how the cat is "related" to the moon in its changeability. So (**d**) is the answer we want.

Q9. The poet only uses three types of punctuation to end the lines in this poem. Which of these punctuation marks does he NOT use throughout the poem?

a) **Question mark**
b) **Comma**
c) **Semicolon**
d) **Full stop**

Answer: C

This is an "odd one out" type of question where we need to find something that has NOT been used, rather than something that is there in front of us. So to answer this question, we need to look carefully through the poem and concentrate on the punctuation the poet has used. We can count three question marks, so the answer is not (**a**). Looking next for commas, we can find 16 of them! So (**b**) is similarly incorrect. Now for (**c**), semicolons. On close inspection, there are none to be seen in the poem. Just to make sure, we can look for full stops, and there are six of them. So (**d**) is excluded too, and we can be certain that the right option is (**c**).

Q10. Why do you think the poet uses the word "changing" twice within the last two lines?

a) To finish the poem by emphasising the similarities between the moon and the cat
b) To simply make a repetitive noise when the poem is read aloud
c) The poet had run out of things to say so just used the same word
d) The poet made an error of literary style

Answer: A

Again, with a "why do you think?" question, we are looking for the most likely answer. Options **(c)** and **(d)** are very unlikely indeed, as when a poet repeats a word, he does it deliberately to achieve a particular effect, not because of laziness or error.

Option **(b)** could have some merit, as a poem is usually written to be spoken aloud as well as to be read on the page. We see the poet does use a few words repeatedly in this poem, which helps achieve a certain rhythm: "dance" is used four times and "round", "crescent", "change" and "changing" are all repeated in the last eight lines. But these words are not "simply" repeated for rhythm's sake, so **(b)** is not quite right, and the final two "changing[s]", used to describe the cat's eyes and the moon (which changes slowly every night during the lunar cycle) appear to be applied as adjectives to both the cat and the moon so that we recognise their "kinship" – the main subject of the poem – which the poet emphasises in the final lines. So the most likely answer is **(a)**.

The Extended Concentration Paper

The extended concentration paper in many ways resembles the scattershot paper. The key difference is that the extended concentration paper has nearly twice as many questions, and so it requires candidates to keep up their levels of focus over longer periods of time.

You will notice also that there are questions about more niche language techniques in these extended concentration papers. These are questions that are less likely to come up, but are modelled on questions that one does occasionally see in 11+ papers. In other words, if you can cope with the range of questions in the extended concentration paper, you will be well equipped to face any challenge the 11+ examiners might throw your way!

Paper Seven: Clayhanger
EXTENDED CONCENTRATION PAPER; DIFFICULT;
50 MINUTES

This excerpt, from the first chapter of the book, comes at the end of young Edwin Clayhanger's last day at school, when he has his whole future stretching ahead of him.

1   It was a breezy Friday in July 1872. The canal, which ran north and south, reflected a blue and white sky. Towards the bridge, from the north came a long narrow canal-boat roofed with tarpaulins; and towards the bridge, from the south came a similar craft, sluggishly creeping. The towing-path was a morass of sticky brown mud, for, in
5   the way of rain, that year was breaking the records of a century and a half. Thirty yards in front of each boat an unhappy skeleton of a horse floundered its best in the quagmire. The honest endeavour of one of the animals received a frequent tonic from a bare-legged girl of seven who heartily curled a whip about its crooked large-jointed legs. The ragged and filthy child danced in the rich mud round the horse's
10 flanks with the simple joy of one who had been rewarded for good behaviour by the unrestricted use of a whip for the first time.

Edwin, with his elbows on the stone parapet of the bridge, stared uninterested at the spectacle of the child, the whip, and the skeleton. He was not insensible to the piquancy of the pageant of life, but his mind was preoccupied with grave and heavy
15 matters. He had left school that day, and what his eyes saw as he leaned on the bridge was not a willing beast and a gladdened infant, but the puzzling world and the

advance guard of its problems bearing down on him. Slim, gawky, untidy, fair, with his worn black-braided clothes, and slung over his shoulders in a bursting satchel the last load of his schoolbooks, and on his bright, rough hair a shapeless cap whose lining protruded behind, he had the extraordinary wistful look of innocence and simplicity which marks most boys of sixteen. It seemed rather a shame, it seemed even tragic, that this naïve, simple creature, with his straightforward and friendly eyes so eager to believe appearances, this creature immaculate of worldly experience, must soon be transformed into a man, wary, incredulous, detracting. Older eyes might have wept at the simplicity of those eyes.

This picture of Edwin as a wistful innocent would have made Edwin laugh. He had been seven years at school, and considered himself a hardened sort of brute, free of illusions. And he sometimes thought that he could judge the world better than most neighbouring mortals.

"Hello! The Sunday!" he murmured, without turning his eyes.

Another boy, a little younger and shorter, and clothed in a superior untidiness, had somehow got on to the bridge, and was leaning with his back against the parapet which supported Edwin's elbows. His eyes were franker and simpler even than the eyes of Edwin, and his lips seemed to be permanently parted in a good-humoured smile. His name was Charlie Orgreave, but at school he was invariably called "the Sunday"—not "Sunday," but "the Sunday"—and nobody could authoritatively explain how he had come by the nickname. Its origin was lost in the prehistoric ages of his childhood. He and Edwin had been chums for several years. They had not sworn fearful oaths of loyalty; they did not constitute a secret society; they had not even pricked forearms and written certain words in blood; for these rites are only performed at Harrow, and possibly at the Oldcastle High School, which imitates Harrow. Their fellowship meant chiefly that they spent a great deal of time together, instinctively and unconsciously enjoying each other's mere presence, and that in public arguments they always reinforced each other, whatever the degree of intellectual dishonesty thereby necessitated.

"I'll bet you mine gets to the bridge first," said the Sunday. With an ingenious movement of the shoulders he arranged himself so that the parapet should bear the weight of his satchel.

Edwin Clayhanger slowly turned round, and perceived that the object which the Sunday had appropriated as "his" was the other canal-boat, advancing from the south.

"Horse or boat?" asked Edwin.

"Boat's nose, of course," said the Sunday.

"Well," said Edwin, having surveyed the unconscious competitors, and counting on the aid of the whipping child, "I don't mind laying you five."

"That be damned for a tale!" protested the Sunday. "We said we'd never bet less than ten—you know that."

"Yes, but—" Edwin hesitatingly drawled.

"But what?"

"All right. Ten," Edwin agreed. "But it's not fair. You've got a rare start on me."

"Rats!" said the Sunday, with finality. In the pronunciation of this word the difference between his accent and Edwin's came out clear. The Sunday's accent was less local; there was a hint of a short "e" sound in the "a," and a briskness about the consonants, that Edwin could never have compassed. The Sunday's accent was as carelessly superior as his clothes. Evidently the Sunday had some one at home who had not learnt the art of speech in the Five Towns.

He began to outline a scheme, in which perpendicular expectoration figured, for accurately deciding the winner, and a complicated argument might have ensued about this, had it not soon become apparent that Edwin's boat was going to be handsomely beaten, despite the joyous efforts of the little child. The horse that would die but would not give up, was only saved from total subsidence at every step by his indomitable if aged spirit. Edwin handed over the ten marbles even before the other boat had arrived at the bridge.

"Here," he said. "And you may as well have these, too," adding five more to the ten, all he possessed. They were not the paltry marble of to-day, plaything of infants, but the majestic "rinker," black with white spots, the king of marbles in an era when whole populations practised the game. Edwin looked at them half regretfully as they lay in the Sunday's hands. They seemed prodigious wealth in those hands, and he felt somewhat as a condemned man might feel who bequeaths his jewels on the scaffold. Then there was a rattle, and a tumour grew out larger on the Sunday's thigh.

An extract from Clayhanger by Arnold Bennett.

Q1. What was the weather like on the day described?

   a) Stormy
   b) Cold and rainy

c) Breezy
d) Hot and humid

Answer: ___

Q2. The canal boat from the south was "sluggishly creeping". What does the writer mean by this?

a) The boat was going much faster than any other boat
b) The boat was not moving at all
c) The boat had got stuck to the banks of the canal
d) The boat was moving very slowly

Answer: ___

Q3. The words "morass" in line 4 and "quagmire" in line 7 are synonyms (words that mean the same) in this extract. What is another word with the same meaning?

a) Flood
b) Swamp
c) Boat
d) Bridge

Answer: ___

Q4. How far in front of the boats were the horses which pulled them?

a) The horses were level with the boats
b) The horses were behind the boats
c) The horses were thirty yards in front of the boats
d) The horses were thirty metres in front of the boats

Answer: ___

Q5. Why do you think the writer describes the horses as "large-jointed"?

a) The horses were so thin that their joints looked large in comparison to their thin legs
b) The horses were particularly large and therefore so were their joints
c) Canal horses are specially bred to have very large joints in their legs
d) The "joints" refer to the carpentry joints on the wooden canal boats

Answer: ___

Q6. When the writer refers to a horse as "the skeleton" in line 13 he is using a figure of speech. Is it:

a) A simile
b) An understatement
c) Alliteration
d) A metaphor

Answer: ___

Q7. What does the author mean when he writes "the piquancy of the pageant of life" at lines 13-14?

a) The boredom of life's ordinary path
b) The excitement of the different things to see in life
c) The stress and fear of life's hardships
d) The pitiful tragedies that can happen in life

Answer: ___

Q8. In line 17 the writer describes Edwin as "slim, gawky, untidy, fair…" What three words does he use to describe the man Edwin "must" become?

a) Wistful, simple, innocent.
b) Grave, preoccupied, heavy.
c) Uninterested, rough, shapeless.
d) Wary, incredulous, detracting.

Answer: ___

Q9. The writer has a style that contains a generous use of adjectives. Which of these words is NOT an adjective as used in this passage?

a) Immaculate
b) Protruded
c) Black-braided
d) Hardened

Answer: ___

Q10. What was The Sunday's real name?

a) Edwin Clayhanger
b) Edwin Orgreave
c) Charlie Orgreave
d) Charlie Sunday

Answer: ___

Q11. How many years had Edwin spent at school?

a) Fourteen years
b) Twelve years
c) Ten years
d) Seven years

Answer: ___

Q12. What is another word that means "rites" as in line 40?

a) Rituals
b) Sporting events
c) Dramas
d) Church services

Answer: ___

Q13. In lines 43-45 the author writes "In public arguments they [the two boys] always reinforced each other, whatever the degree of intellectual dishonesty thereby necessitated". What does this mean?

a) The two boys always took different sides in public arguments.
b) The two boys always backed each other up in public, but argued constantly in private.
c) The two boys always supported each other publicly, even if they had to be untruthful to do so.
d) The two boys never entered into public arguments; they would rather be untruthful than do so.

Answer: ___

Q14. Which words in the passage tell us that Edwin and The Sunday often made bets with each other?

a) "Horse or boat?"
b) "Rats! said The Sunday"
c) "I don't mind laying you five"
d) "We said we'd never bet less than ten – you know that"

Answer: ___

Q15. What does the adjective "unconscious" mean in line 54 where it is used to describe the noun "competitors"?

a) It means that the people on the boat are fast asleep
b) It means that the boat crews and their horses are unaware of being the subjects of a bet
c) It means that somebody has attacked and knocked out everyone on the boats
d) It means that the horses pulling the boats are so exhausted that they are only semi-conscious

Answer: ___

Q16. How do we know that Edwin and The Sunday come from different backgrounds?

a) The Sunday is younger and more innocent than Edwin
b) The Sunday wears neater clothes than Edwin does
c) Edwin is prepared to bet more money than The Sunday
d) The Sunday has a different accent to Edwin

Answer: ___

Q17. What would Edwin's reaction be to the picture of himself as a "wistful innocent"?

a) It would make him very angry
b) It would seem funny to him
c) He would agree with it wholeheartedly
d) It would completely confuse him

Answer: ___

Q18. What is the object of this sentence: "The ragged and filthy child danced in the rich mud"?

a) The rich mud
b) The child
c) Danced
d) Ragged and filthy

Answer: ___

Q19. What type of words are the following: "mine"; "his"; "you"; "they"?

a) Conjunctions
b) Nouns
c) Pronouns
d) Prepositions

Answer: ___

Q20. What is another word with the same meaning as "appropriated" in line 50?

a) Approval
b) Taken
c) Disliked
d) Discarded

Answer: ___

Q21. The Sunday says to Edwin "We said we'd never bet less than ten – you know that." Ten what?

a) Ten pence
b) Ten sweets
c) Ten marbles
d) Ten pounds

Answer: ___

Q22. How did The Sunday get his nickname?

a) He attended Sunday school as a small boy.
b) Edwin only met up with him on Sundays
c) His surname was Sunday
d) Nobody remembered how he got the nickname

Answer: ___

Q23. What is a "parapet" in line 12?

a) A small parachute that landed on the bridge
b) The part of a bridge that is underwater
c) A stone barrier to stop people falling from a bridge
d) A canal boat towed by a horse

Answer: ___

Q24. Which of these words from the extract is NOT an adverb?

a) Hesitatingly
b) Friendly
c) Heartily
d) Handsomely

Answer: ___

Q25. What did Edwin carry in his satchel?

a) His school books
b) His packed lunch
c) Homework for that night
d) Nothing but marbles

Answer: ___

Q26. Which of these statements is true?

a) Edwin won the bet on the boats
b) Nobody won the bet, because it was a tie between the two boats
c) The Sunday won the bet on the boats
d) The boats never reached the bridge

Answer: ___

Q27. Edwin "hesitatingly drawled" in line 58. What is the meaning of the verb to drawl?

a) To cry out in a panic
b) To whisper nervously
c) To speak slowly and lazily
d) To shout angrily

Answer: ___

Q28. What type of words are the following: "similar"; "sticky"; "unrestricted"; "tragic"; "superior"?

a) Adverbs
b) Verbs
c) Prepositions
d) Adjectives

Answer: ___

Q29. What does the author mean when he refers to the "joyous efforts of the little child" in line 70?

a) Her dancing in the mud
b) Her whipping of the horse
c) Her effort to win the bet
d) Her effort to get to the bridge first

Answer: ___

Q30. What expression was usually on The Sunday's face?

a) A good-humoured smile
b) An ill-natured scowl
c) A confused frown
d) A bored sneer

Answer: ___

Q31. What tense is used in this extract?

a) The present tense

b) The future tense
c) The past tense
d) None of the above

Answer: ___

Q32. What does the word "ensued" mean in line 68?

a) Ended
b) Never happened
c) Broken
d) Followed

Answer: ___

Q33. "He felt somewhat as a condemned man might feel" at lines 78-79 is an example of:

a) A simile
b) Alliteration
c) A metaphor
d) Personification

Answer: ___

Q34. What is the name of the marble the writer calls "majestic"?

a) The King
b) The Sunday
c) The Twinkler
d) The Rinker

Answer: ___

Q35. Which of these statements is true?

a) Edwin and The Sunday had formed a secret society
b) Edwin and The Sunday had sworn an oath of loyalty
c) Edwin and The Sunday had been friends for a long time
d) Edwin and The Sunday did not spend much time together

Answer: ___

Q36. How old is Edwin Clayhanger in this extract?

a) Nineteen
b) Sixteen
c) Fourteen
d) Ten

Answer: ___

Q37. After the words "tarpaulins", "loyalty", "society", "blood" and "local" in this passage, there is a punctuation mark. What is it called?

a) A question mark
b) An exclamation point
c) A semicolon
d) A full stop

Answer: ___

Q38. What is another word that means the same as "prodigious" in line 78?

a) Little
b) Impressive
c) Meaningless
d) Invisible

Answer: ___

Q39. "Then there was a rattle, and a tumour grew out larger on The Sunday's thigh."

What figure of speech is used in this sentence?

a) A simile
b) A metaphor
c) Hyphoria
d) Alliteration

Answer: ___

Q40. Which of these statements matches the end of the extract?

a) Edwin had won the bet and The Sunday paid him the ten marbles he had lost
b) The Sunday had won the bet but Edwin refused to pay him the ten marbles
c) The bet was a draw, so nobody lost or won any marbles at all
d) The Sunday won the bet and Edwin gave him all the marbles he owned

Answer: ___

Paper Seven: Answers & Guidance

Q1. What was the weather like on the day described?

a) Stormy
b) Cold and rainy
c) Breezy
d) Hot and humid

Answer: C

We start off the paper with a clear and simple retrieval question, to which the answer can be found at the beginning of the extract in line 1: "It was a breezy Friday in July 1872". So the right answer is **(c)**.

Q2. The canal boat from the south was "sluggishly creeping". What does the writer mean by this?

a) The boat was going much faster than any other boat
b) The boat was not moving at all
c) The boat had got stuck to the banks of the canal
d) The boat was moving very slowly

Answer: D

A slug is a small garden creature, like a snail but without a shell. It crawls around, having no legs, so is known for its lack of speed. Therefore to move "sluggishly" is to be slow. When this adverb is accompanied by the verb "creeping", which indicates careful, measured movement, the meaning becomes clear. So the correct option here is (**d**).

If there is any doubt, we can go back to the text and exclude the other options: we know the boat was actually moving, or the boys could not have bet on its progress, so (**b**) and (**c**) cannot be right. Nor can (**a**), since if one boat was obviously much faster than any other, there would be no point betting against it.

Q3. The words "morass" in line 4 and "quagmire" in line 7 are synonyms (words that mean the same) in this extract. What is another word with the same meaning?

    a) Flood
    b) Swamp
    c) Boat
    d) Bridge

Answer: B

Here we have a vocabulary question which gives us two relatively unusual words with the same meaning, and asks us to find a third one. Reading the text where the two words occur, we can see that the "towing path" (the path on the banks of the canal where the horses walk) is described in detail. So we can pick up evidence to let us get to the correct answer.

Firstly, only the towing path is described as "a morass", not a boat or the bridge, so we must reject answers (**c**) and (**d**). (**a**) is more of a possibility, so to choose between (**a**) and (**b**) we can spot two expressions that also depict the towpath: "sticky brown mud" and "the rich mud around the horses' flanks" (flanks refer to the underside of the horse). If the towpath was flooded, the horses would be wading through water, but they are in sticky mud, which is typical of a swamp. So (**b**) is the correct answer.

. . .

Q4. How far in front of the boats were the horses which pulled them?

a) The horses were level with the boats
b) The horses were behind the boats
c) The horses were thirty yards in front of the boats
d) The horses were thirty metres in front of the boats

Answer: C

A simpler question here which can be answered by looking at lines 5-6 in the extract: "Thirty yards in front of each boat an unhappy skeleton of a horse floundered..." However, eliminating the other answers is a useful exercise.

If the horses were level with, or behind the boats, they could not tow them along. So we can eliminate options **(a)** and **(b)**. This text is from a book set in 19th century England, and metric measurements (metres, centimetres etc) have only been used in England since the 1960s. So **(d)** would not be possible in 1872, and we can confirm that **(c)** is the right option here.

Q5. Why do you think the writer describes the horses as "large-jointed"?

a) The horses were so thin that their joints looked large in comparison to their thin legs
b) The horses were particularly large and therefore so were their joints
c) Canal horses are specially bred to have very large joints in their legs
d) The "joints" refer to the carpentry joints on the wooden canal boats

Answer: A

This question is asking for our interpretation of the writer's intent, so we are looking for the most likely answer here. Firstly, let us reject answer **(d)** as lines 8-9 directly refers to the "crooked, large-jointed legs" of the *horse*, not the boat. Moving up, answer **(c)** is unlikely because breeding especially large, bulging joints would make the horses' performance more painful and less strong. Answer **(b)** is also not convincing because the size of the horse was not important compared to its stamina and perseverance. In fact barges were often pulled by small, strong ponies, donkeys or mules. So – given that we know the writer has compared the skinny, "aged" horse to a skeleton, which is nothing but bones and joints – **(a)** seems the most likely answer.

Q6. When the writer refers to a horse as "the skeleton" in line 13 he is using a figure of speech. Is it:

    a) **A simile**
    b) **An understatement**
    c) **Alliteration**
    d) **A metaphor**

Answer: D

Edwin stares at "The child, the whip, and the skeleton". The child and the whip are literally a child and a whip, but the "skeleton" is not literally a skeleton; it is a reference to the horse itself, and as the writer does not say "the horse that was like a skeleton" or a similar construction, he is not using a simile. Nor is he using understatement, which employs minimisation – so if he was using it, the writer might describe the horse as "fairly slim" or something like that.

As for alliteration, that requires the use of at least two words beginning with the same letter, but we do not have that here. So we have eliminated all options except **(d)**, which is correct. A metaphor compares one thing to another in a way that does not need any other qualification.

Q7. What does the author mean when he writes "the piquancy of the pageant of life" at lines 13-14?

    a) The boredom of life's ordinary path
    b) The excitement of the different things to see in life
    c) The stress and fear of life's hardships
    d) The pitiful tragedies that can happen in life

Answer: B

Paper Seven: Answers & Guidance

"Piquancy" means an interesting spiciness, and "pageant" means a colourful parade of different entertainments, so the right answer here is **(b)**; all the other answers are too negative to make sense in the text.

Q8. In line 17 the writer describes Edwin as "slim, gawky, untidy, fair…" What three words does he use to describe the man Edwin "must" become?

a) Wistful, simple, innocent.
b) Grave, preoccupied, heavy.
c) Uninterested, rough, shapeless.
d) Wary, incredulous, detracting.

Answer: D

We are back to a retrieval question again. However, there are some red herrings here, as *all* the adjectives used in the answers here are used by the writer in the passage. So reverting to the text to check, we can find at lines 23-24 the words "[Edwin] must be transformed into a man, wary, incredulous, detracting." Incredulous means unwilling to believe in much and detracting means likely to belittle things in life. **(d)** is the right answer.

Q9. The writer has a style that contains a generous use of adjectives. Which of these words is NOT an adjective as used in this passage?

a) Immaculate
b) Protruded
c) Black-braided
d) Hardened

Answer: B

We can find where the these words are used, and see *how* they are used too. **(a)** Immaculate can be found at line 23 and describes a noun, "creature", so it is certainly an adjective. **(b)** Protruded can be found at line 20 in the clause "…whose lining protruded behind," and it does NOT appear to be describing a noun, but acting as a verb. Just to make sure that it is the non-adjective beyond any doubt, we can find **(c)** Black-braided at line 18 describing Edwin's clothes, and **(d)** Hardened at line 27 describing Edwin's image of himself. Both are used as adjectives, so we know that option **(b)** "protruded" is the correct one here.

Q10. What was The Sunday's real name?

    a) **Edwin Clayhanger**
    b) **Edwin Orgreave**
    c) **Charlie Orgreave**
    d) **Charlie Sunday**

                                                                         Answer: C

This first of two comparatively straightforward retrieval questions needs us to check the excerpt at line 35 where we find: "His [The Sunday's] name was Charlie Orgreave…". So the right answer is **(c)**.

Q11. How many years had Edwin spent at school?

    a) **Fourteen years**
    b) **Twelve years**
    c) **Ten years**
    d) **Seven years**

                                                                          Answer: D

Again, we need to read the text at lines 26-27: "He had been seven years at school…"

Many children started formal school later in the 19th century than they do nowadays, and left school earlier. The right answer here is **(d)**.

Q12. What is another word that means "rites" as in line 40?

    a) **Rituals**

b) **Sporting events**
c) **Dramas**
d) **Church services**

Answer: A

The word "rite" is defined in the dictionary as meaning a solemn act, observance or ceremony. Another synonym for rite is "ritual", so the correct answer to this question is option **(a)**.

Q13. In lines 43-45 the author writes "In public arguments they [the two boys] always reinforced each other, whatever the degree of intellectual dishonesty thereby necessitated". What does this mean?

a) **The two boys always took different sides in public arguments.**
b) **The two boys always backed each other up in public, but argued constantly in private.**
c) **The two boys always supported each other publicly, even if they had to be untruthful to do so.**
d) **The two boys never entered into public arguments; they would rather be untruthful than do so.**

Answer: C

In this sentence from the extract, the writer has used a deliberately complicated construction to say something fairly straightforward. This is done to produce an amusing effect, emphasised by the use of the euphemism (a mild or inoffensive expression replacing something that might be too blunt or strong) of "intellectual dishonesty" instead of saying "telling lies". "Reinforcing" means supporting or strengthening, and "necessitated" means made necessary. So if we deconstruct the whole sentence, we have: "The two boys always supported each other in arguments with other people, even if they had to tell lies to appear to agree with each other." In other words, **(c)** is the right answer.

Q14. Which words in the passage tell us that Edwin and The Sunday ~~ade bets with each other?

a) "Horse or boat?"
b) "Rats! said The Sunday"
c) "I don't mind laying you five"
d) "We said we'd never bet less than ten – you know that"

Answer: D

The first three options here do not tell us anything about previous bets the boys may have made with each other. But lines 56-57 — "We said we'd never bet less than ten – you know that" — tells us that Edwin and The Sunday have already discussed the minimum amount they should agree to bet each other, before the events described in the extract. This implies betting is something they have done before at least once, if not many times. So the answer to the question is (**d**).

Q15. What does the adjective "unconscious" mean in line 54 where it is used to describe the noun "competitors"?

a) It means that the people on the boat are fast asleep
b) It means that the boat crews and their horses are unaware of being the subjects of a bet
c) It means that somebody has attacked and knocked out everyone on the boats
d) It means that the horses pulling the boats are so exhausted that they are only semi-conscious

Answer: B

The word "unconscious" as an adjective can mean asleep, senseless or knocked out. It can also mean, as it does here, unaware of what is going on. The correct answer here is (**b**) as nobody on the boats is aware that they are the subject of a bet between the two boys.

As usual, if unsure of the answer, we can look at the other options and find reasons to reject them. Option (**a**) would be unlikely and very dangerous, as someone has to be awake aboard a boat in order to be in charge and steer it! Option (**c**) must be excluded for the same reasons. Option (**d**) does not make sense here, as even if the writer was only referring to the horses, semi-conscious means half conscious, not unconscious, and if the horses were asleep the boats would not be moving at all. So we are safe in choosing our option **(b)**.

Q16. How do we know that Edwin and The Sunday come from different backgrounds?

    a) The Sunday is younger and more innocent than Edwin
    b) The Sunday wears neater clothes than Edwin does
    c) Edwin is prepared to bet more money than The Sunday
    d) The Sunday has a different accent to Edwin

Answer: D

The first option is technically true, as we know from line 31, where it says that "The Sunday is younger and shorter than Edwin". However, The Sunday's age and height do not tell us anything about his family or background, so this answer is not relevant. The answer **(b)** is actually untrue in the text, where we are told The Sunday was "clothed in a superior untidiness" compared to Edwin, meaning he was dressed in a less neat way than the other boy.

Answer **(c)** is also misleading, as it is Edwin in line 55 who wants to bet only five, rather than the ten that The Sunday reminds him he had agreed to previously when they made bets. However, this is immaterial, since the amount they bet does not give us an insight into their backgrounds.

So **(d)** is the right answer, as told to us by the writer in lines 61 to 66. It is their accents that tell us that they come from different backgrounds.

Q17. What would Edwin's reaction be to the picture of himself as a "wistful innocent"?

    a) It would make him very angry
    b) It would seem funny to him
    c) He would agree with it wholeheartedly
    d) It would completely confuse him

Answer: B

This answer can be retrieved from reading the text at line 26: "This picture of Edwin as a wistful innocent would have made Edwin laugh." Laughter comes when something seems funny, so the correct answer is (**b**).

Q18. What is the object of this sentence: "The ragged and filthy child danced in the rich mud"?

a) The rich mud
b) The child
c) Danced
d) Ragged and filthy

Answer: A

The <u>subject</u> of a sentence is the one that performs the action, and the <u>object</u> of a sentence is acted *upon* and takes the more passive role. In the sentence we have here, answer (**b**), the child, is the subject of the sentence because she is doing the action. Answer (**c**) is the verb or action being performed, and answer (**d**) contains the adjectives used to describe the subject. So we are left with (**a**), the rich mud, which is the object of the sentence and the right answer.

Q19. What type of words are the following: "mine"; "his"; "you"; "they"?

a) Conjunctions
b) Nouns
c) Pronouns
d) Prepositions

Answer: C

These words from the text are all pronouns, so the correct answer is (**c**). Pronouns are used in place of nouns where the constant repetition of the nouns themselves would become ridiculous or make sentences unnecessarily long and complicated. "You" and "They" are simple <u>personal pronouns</u>, and "Mine" and "His" are <u>possessive pronouns</u>, showing ownership.

Paper Seven: Answers & Guidance

. . .

Q20. What is another word with the same meaning as "appropriated" in line 50?

a) Approval
b) Taken
c) Disliked
d) Discarded

Answer: B

If the word is unknown to us, we must examine the text to see which is the most likely word to match it.

The text says "The object which The Sunday had appropriated as 'his' was the other canal boat…" so the word we are looking for, like "appropriated" is a verb in the past tense. **(a)** is a noun, not a verb, so we can reject that. **(c)** and **(d)** are indeed verbs in the correct tense, but their meaning is opposite to what occurs in the text. We know The Sunday chose his boat and took it as "his" one of the two boats to bet on, so **(b)** is the best answer.

Q21. The Sunday says to Edwin "We said we'd never bet less than ten – you know that." Ten what?

a) Ten pence
b) Ten sweets
c) Ten marbles
d) Ten pounds

Answer: C

The writer teases us a little by just saying the number "ten" when the amount the boys will bet is first mentioned, so we might wonder "ten what?" However, in lines 72-73 we are told: "Edwin handed over the ten marbles even before the other boat had arrived at the bridge." So **(c)** is the correct option.

The game of marbles, played with coloured glass balls, was very popular when this text was written. However, ten old pence would have been a lot for boys to bet in the nineteenth century, and as for ten pounds when this novel was written – that would be the equivalent of two schoolboys betting £1,263 today!

Q22. How did The Sunday get his nickname?

    a) He attended Sunday school as a small boy.
    b) Edwin only met up with him on Sundays
    c) His surname was Sunday
    d) Nobody remembered how he got the nickname

Answer: D

We can retrieve the answer to this question by finding lines 36-37 in the passage: "— and nobody could authoritatively [reliably and accurately] explain how he had come by the nickname."

So we can see the right answer is (**d**).

Q23. What is a "parapet" in line 12?

    a) A small parachute that landed on the bridge
    b) The part of a bridge that is underwater
    c) A stone barrier to stop people falling from a bridge
    d) A canal boat towed by a horse

Answer: C

If we are not sure of the meaning of the word parapet, it is a good idea to carefully examine the context of the word to make our best attempt at finding the right option here.

The writer uses the word three times in the extract. At line 12 he writes: "Edwin, with his elbows on the stone parapet of the bridge...". At line 32 comes "[The Sunday] was leaning with his back against the parapet..." and at lines 47-48 we see "he arranged himself so that the parapet should bear the weight of his satchel."

With this evidence, we can see that the only possible option is (**c**). The boys could not lean on a parachute – even if there were one in the text, so (**a**) is wrong – nor would they be underwater or on a boat, so (**b**) and (**d**) can be ruled out too.

Q24. Which of these words from the extract is NOT an adverb?

a) **Hesitatingly**
b) **Friendly**
c) **Heartily**
d) **Handsomely**

Answer: B

A vocabulary question which is a little different – it asks us to find the "odd one out", as three of the options are adverbs and one is not. Adverbs describe an action, so a good method here is either to check in the extract how each word is used, or, if short of time, we could apply all the words to one verb, and see which works and which does not.

Let us take the verb "spoke" and try the options with it. "They spoke hesitatingly" works. "They spoke heartily" works too, as does "They spoke handsomely". So we can be sure these are all adverbs. However, "They spoke friendly" does not make grammatical sense. Despite ending with "ly", friendly is a red herring and only describes nouns. So it is an adjective, *not* an adverb, and the correct answer to the question is therefore (**b**).

Q25. What did Edwin carry in his satchel?

a) **His school books**
b) **His packed lunch**
c) **Homework for that night**
d) **Nothing but marbles**

Answer: A

We can find the answer at lines 18-19 in the extract: "...slung over his shoulders in a bursting satchel the last load of his school-books..."; accordingly, option **(a)** is the right one here. It doesn't sound as if there was room for anything else!

Q26. Which of these statements is true?

    a) Edwin won the bet on the boats
    b) Nobody won the bet, because it was a tie between the two boats
    c) The Sunday won the bet on the boats
    d) The boats never reached the bridge

Answer: C

"...had it not soon become apparent that Edwin's boat was going to be handsomely beaten..." comes at lines 69-70 and tells us that The Sunday won the bet the boys made. If there was any doubt, the writer confirms the result, by saying Edwin paid The Sunday the marbles he owed before Edwin's boat had even arrived at the bridge. So the correct answer is **(c)**.

Q27. Edwin "hesitatingly drawled" in line 58. What is the meaning of the verb to drawl?

    a) To cry out in a panic
    b) To whisper nervously
    c) To speak slowly and lazily
    d) To shout angrily

Answer: C

To "drawl" is to speak slowly and lazily, drawing out your words and making them longer than normal. So **(c)** is the right answer. The other definitions given as options are not relevant to the text, as there is no reason that Edwin would be crying out in panic, whispering or angrily shouting during a relaxed time with his friend.

. . .

Q28. What type of words are the following: "similar"; "sticky"; "unrestricted"; "tragic"; "superior"?

a) Adverbs
b) Verbs
c) Prepositions
d) Adjectives

Answer: D

These words taken from the excerpt are all words that describe nouns, so they are adjectives and the right answer is (**d**). "Unrestricted" describes something that has no limits.

Q29. What does the author mean when he refers to the "joyous efforts of the little child" in line 70?

a) Her dancing in the mud
b) Her whipping of the horse
c) Her effort to win the bet
d) Her effort to get to the bridge first

Answer: B

The adjective "joyous" is derived from the noun "joy", and we have read in lines 9-11 that "The ragged and filthy child danced in the rich mud round the horse's flanks with the simple <u>joy</u> of one who had been rewarded for good behaviour by the unrestricted use of the whip for the first time".

Whatever we might think about the treatment of animals at the time, we know that the whipping of the horse made the child joyous, so (**b**) is the correct answer.

Q30. What expression was usually on The Sunday's face?

a) A good-humoured smile
b) An ill-natured scowl

c) A confused frown
d) A bored sneer

Answer: A

The negative and quite unpleasant facial expressions contained in answers **(b)**, **(c)** and **(d)** do not seem to fit the character of The Sunday as written in this passage; and if we read lines 34-35 we can see "his lips seemed to be permanently parted in a good-humoured smile". So we can be certain the answer is **(a)**.

Q31. What tense is used in this extract?

a) The present tense
b) The future tense
c) The past tense
d) None of the above

Answer: C

Almost every verb we can pick out from the passage, such as "ran", "reflected", "floundered", "lost" and so on, is in the past tense. The novel from which this extract is taken is set in 1872, as we read in line 1. The novel was not published until 1910, and has the atmosphere of a reminiscence (a memory or narrative of past events). So with this evidence, we can conclude that the right option here is **(c)**.

Q32. What does the word "ensued" mean in line 68?

a) Ended
b) Never happened
c) Broken
d) Followed

Answer: D

In the text we can find the following quote: "...a complicated argument might have ensued about this..."

If we do not know the meaning of the word "ensued", we could try inserting all the options we have been given, to see which makes sense in the context of the story. An argument has not begun, so it cannot be ended, so option **(a)** is wrong. Similarly, options **(b)** and **(c)** do not fit into the sentence in a meaningful way. However, option **(d)** seems to fit in well: "A complicated argument might have followed after this", so we can confirm that **(d)** is the correct answer.

Q33. "He felt somewhat as a condemned man might feel" at lines 78-79 is an example of:

a) A simile
b) Alliteration
c) A metaphor
d) Personification

Answer: A

In literature, when one thing is compared to another with the use of "as" or "like", it is an example of a simile. So answer **(a)** is the correct one, because Edwin is feeling *as* a condemned man (a man sentenced to death for a crime and awaiting his punishment) might feel. It is rather an exaggerated simile, since the condemned man Edwin imagines has given away all his jewels, whereas he himself has given away only marbles; but the writer, by using the simile, helps us to understand Edwin's sensitive and rather dramatic nature.

As an aside: technically speaking, a simile is a type of metaphor; so in a sense, you could argue that **(c)** ought to be considered a correct answer, too. However, when the comparison from the extract makes use of "as" or "like", the mark scheme will always be looking for 'simile' as opposed to 'metaphor' – so just swallow that urge to argue on a technicality and opt for simile!

Q34. What is the name of the marble the writer calls "majestic"?

a) The King
b) The Sunday
c) The Twinkler

d) **The Rinker**

Answer: D

A straightforward retrieval question here, which can be read at line 76: "...the majestic 'rinker', black with white spots, the king of marbles...". So we must go for answer **(d)**.

Q35. Which of these statements is true?

a) **Edwin and The Sunday had formed a secret society**
b) **Edwin and The Sunday had sworn an oath of loyalty**
c) **Edwin and The Sunday had been friends for a long time**
d) **Edwin and The Sunday did not spend much time together**

Answer: C

If unsure of the answer to this question, we can go through the options and find evidence for or against each of them. At lines 38-39 we see: "They [Edwin and The Sunday] had not sworn fearful oaths of loyalty; they did not constitute (form) a secret society…"; so we can reject **(a)** and **(b)** as possible answers.

(d) immediately seems wrong, and at line 42 the writer says "...they [Edwin and The Sunday] spent a great deal of time together", which confirms that **(d)** is incorrect.

We are left, then, with the true statement contained in answer **(c)**, which we can find evidence for at line 38: "He [The Sunday] and Edwin had been chums for several years." The word chums means friends and is old-fashioned now, but was in common usage until quite recently.

Q36. How old is Edwin Clayhanger in this extract?

a) **Nineteen**
b) **Sixteen**
c) **Fourteen**
d) **Ten**

Paper Seven: Answers & Guidance

Answer: B

In lines 20-21 we read that "[Edwin] had the extraordinary wistful look of innocence and simplicity which marks most boys of sixteen." So the correct option here is **(b)**. Sons of working-class parents at the time generally left school at sixteen to be apprenticed in a trade or work in the family business. Higher education was mostly for the wealthy or the especially gifted.

Q37. After the words "tarpaulins", "loyalty", "society", "blood" and "local" in this passage, there is a punctuation mark. What is it called?

a) A question mark
b) An exclamation point
c) A semicolon
d) A full stop

Answer: C

Examining the relevant part of the text, we can see the same punctuation mark follows all the words in the question. It is a semicolon, which means the right answer is **(c)**.

Q38. What is another word that means the same as "prodigious" in line 78?

a) Little
b) Impressive
c) Meaningless
d) Invisible

Answer: B

The word "prodigious" is defined as remarkably great or large in extent, and in its context within the extract only option **(b)** can be correct, since all the other answers are negative ones. The marbles seemed "prodigious wealth" to Edwin, once he had given them away to The Sunday; indeed, many things seem more desirable once we have lost them.

Q39. "Then there was a rattle, and a tumour grew out larger on The Sunday's thigh."

What figure of speech is used in this sentence?

   a) **A simile**
   b) **A metaphor**
   c) **Hyphoria**
   d) **Alliteration**

Answer: B

There is no alliteration (two or more words beginning with the same letter) in the sentence in the question, so **(d)** is incorrect.

Hyphoria is when a writer asks a question, then instantly answers it himself/herself. Accordingly, we can eliminate **(c)** as well.

A tumour is a lump or swelling, often indicating ill health, but here we have two healthy boys of sixteen, so the "tumour" is actually used by the writer to describe the bump made in The Sunday's thigh by all the marbles he has won, tumbling and rattling into his now lumpy trouser pocket. If the writer had said "it seemed as if a tumour grew out" or "it looked like a tumour grew out" then the figure of speech would be a simile. But there is no such qualification and one thing (the bulge the marbles made) is directly called another thing "a tumour". As a result, answer **(a)** is wrong and answer **(b)** is correct; it is a metaphor.

Q40. Which of these statements matches the end of the extract?

   a) **Edwin had won the bet and The Sunday paid him the ten marbles he had lost**
   b) **The Sunday had won the bet but Edwin refused to pay him the ten marbles**
   c) **The bet was a draw, so nobody lost or won any marbles at all**

d) The Sunday won the bet and Edwin gave him all the marbles he owned

Answer: D

We are being asked to decide which of the answers best matches the end of the comprehension passage, and to make sure we end the paper with a good answer, we can go through the options with a process of elimination and show the examiner we have understood the narrative.

Option **(a)** immediately looks incorrect as we have established that The Sunday won the bet on the boats. We saw in lines 69-70 that "...Edwin's boat was going to be handsomely beaten..." and also that Edwin gave The Sunday marbles, not the other way around. So **(a)** is incorrect.

Option **(b)** correctly says The Sunday won the bet, but then suggests that Edwin refused to pay him any marbles. We know this is untrue, as in lines 72-73 we see "Edwin handed over the ten marbles even before the other boat had arrived at the bridge." So **(b)** is another wrong answer. Actually, Edwin pays The Sunday more than he strictly owes him.

Option **(c)** has no support in the text whatsoever, as we know the bet was won and the debt paid.

So we come to option **(d)** and by sheer elimination we know it must be correct, but it is also backed up by many lines in the text. If you got this last question right, congratulations for understanding the narrative and for reaching the end of a long paper!

Paper Eight: The Mill on the Floss
EXTENDED CONCENTRATION PAPER; DEVILISH;
50 MINUTES

This extract is from a novel set in the early 19th Century in Lincolnshire, and follows the Tulliver family, who run a water-mill. Here young Tom Tulliver returns to school to find he will be studying with the son of a local lawyer, the man his father hates.

---

1   "Well, Tulliver, we're glad to see you again," said Mr Stelling, heartily. "Take off your wrappings and come into the study till dinner. You'll find a bright fire there, and a new companion."

Tom felt in an uncomfortable flutter as he took off his woollen comforter and other
5   wrappings. He had seen Philip Wakem at St Ogg's, but had always turned his eyes away from him as quickly as possible. He would have disliked having a deformed boy for his companion, even if Philip had not been the son of a bad man. And Tom did not see how a bad man's son could be very good. His own father was a good man, and he would readily have fought any one who said the contrary. He was in a state of
10   mingled embarrassment and defiance as he followed Mr Stelling to the study.

"Here is a new companion for you to shake hands with, Tulliver," said that gentleman on entering the study,—"Master Philip Wakem. I shall leave you to make acquaintance by yourselves. You already know something of each other, I imagine; for you are neighbours at home."

15 Tom looked confused and awkward, while Philip rose and glanced at him timidly. Tom did not like to go up and put out his hand, and he was not prepared to say, "How do you do?" on so short a notice.

Mr Stelling wisely turned away, and closed the door behind him; boys' shyness only wears off in the absence of their elders.

20 Philip was at once too proud and too timid to walk toward Tom. He thought, or rather felt, that Tom had an aversion to looking at him; every one, almost, disliked looking at him; and his deformity was more conspicuous when he walked. So they remained without shaking hands or even speaking, while Tom went to the fire and warmed himself, every now and then casting furtive glances at Philip, who seemed to
25 be drawing absently first one object and then another on a piece of paper he had before him. He had seated himself again, and as he drew, was thinking what he could say to Tom, and trying to overcome his own repugnance to making the first advances.

Tom began to look oftener and longer at Philip's face, for he could see it without noticing the hump, and it was really not a disagreeable face,—very old-looking, Tom
30 thought. He wondered how much older Philip was than himself. An anatomist—even a mere physiognomist—would have seen that the deformity of Philip's spine was not a congenital hump, but the result of an accident in infancy; but you do not expect from Tom any acquaintance with such distinctions; to him, Philip was simply a humpback. He had a vague notion that the deformity of Wakem's son had some rela-
35 tion to the lawyer's rascality, of which he had so often heard his father talk with hot emphasis; and he felt, too, a half-admitted fear of him as probably a spiteful fellow, who, not being able to fight you, had cunning ways of doing you a mischief by the sly. There was a humpbacked tailor in the neighbourhood of Mr Jacobs's academy, who was considered a very unamiable character, and was much hooted after by public-
40 spirited boys solely on the ground of his unsatisfactory moral qualities; so that Tom was not without a basis of fact to go upon. Still, no face could be more unlike that ugly tailor's than this melancholy boy's face,—the brown hair round it waved and curled at the ends like a girl's: Tom thought that truly pitiable. This Wakem was a pale, puny fellow, and it was quite clear he would not be able to play at anything
45 worth speaking of; but he handled his pencil in an enviable manner, and was apparently making one thing after another without any trouble. What was he drawing? Tom was quite warm now, and wanted something new to be going forward. It was certainly more agreeable to have an ill-natured humpback as a companion than to stand looking out of the study window at the rain, and kicking his foot against the
50 washboard in solitude; something would happen every day, "a quarrel or something"; and Tom thought he should rather like to show Philip that he had better not try his spiteful tricks on *him*. He suddenly walked across the hearth and looked over Philip's paper.

"Why, that's a donkey with panniers, and a spaniel, and partridges in the corn!" he exclaimed, his tongue being completely loosed by surprise and admiration. "Oh my buttons! I wish I could draw like that. I'm to learn drawing this half; I wonder if I shall learn to make dogs and donkeys!"

"Oh, you can do them without learning," said Philip; "I never learned drawing."

"Never learned?" said Tom, in amazement. "Why, when I make dogs and horses, and those things, the heads and the legs won't come right; though I can see how they ought to be very well. I can make houses, and all sorts of chimneys,—chimneys going all down the wall,—and windows in the roof, and all that. But I dare say I could do dogs and horses if I was to try more," he added, reflecting that Philip might falsely suppose that he was going to "knock under," if he were too frank about the imperfection of his accomplishments.

"Oh, yes," said Philip, "it's very easy. You've only to look well at things, and draw them over and over again. What you do wrong once, you can alter the next time."

"But haven't you been taught *any*thing?" said Tom, beginning to have a puzzled suspicion that Philip's crooked back might be the source of remarkable faculties. "I thought you'd been to school a long while."

"Yes," said Philip, smiling; "I've been taught Latin and Greek and mathematics, and writing and such things." (Philip, you perceive, was not without a wish to impress the well-made barbarian with a sense of his mental superiority.)

"Oh, but I say, you don't like Latin, though, do you?" said Tom, lowering his voice confidentially.

"Pretty well; I don't care much about it," said Philip.

"Ah, but perhaps you haven't got into the "*Propriae quae maribus*" said Tom, nodding his head sideways, as much as to say, "that was the test: it was easy talking until you came to *that.*"

Philip felt some bitter complacency in the promising stupidity of this well-made active-looking boy; but made polite by his own extreme sensitiveness as well as his desire to conciliate, he checked his inclination to laugh, and said quietly,

" I've done with the grammar: I don't learn that any more."

An extract from George Eliot's The Mill on the Floss

Q1. This extract begins with Tom's tutor welcoming him back to school. What is the tutor's name?

a) Stephen Ogg
b) Philip Wakem
c) Mr Stelling
d) Mr Jacobs

Answer: ___

Q2. What two things were awaiting Tom in the study?

a) A bright fire and a hot drink
b) A bright fire and a new companion
c) A comfortable chair and a bright fire
d) A hot drink and a new companion

Answer: ___

Q3. A "comforter" was an old word for a...

a) Scarf
b) Glove
c) Leather boot
d) Cup of tea

Answer: ___

Q4. "Tom did not see how a bad man's son could be very good." Which of the following statements best describes Tom's opinion?

a) A bad man's son could be very good
b) A good man's son is always good
c) A good man's son could be very bad
d) A bad man's son could not be very good

Answer: ___

Q5. Tom was embarrassed as he followed Mr Stelling into the study. What other emotion did he feel?

a) Delight
b) Defiance
c) Confusion
d) Destiny

Answer: ___

Q6. What is the meaning of "to make acquaintance" in lines 12-13?

a) To join in a game
b) To get to know one another
c) To become best friends
d) To study lessons together

Answer: ___

Q7. Why does the writer use the adverb "wisely" of Mr Stelling's exit from the study in line 18?

a) Because Mr Stelling is always wise in everything he does, so he even leaves the room wisely
b) Because Mr Stelling thinks the boys will fight, so he wisely leaves the room as he doesn't want to be involved
c) Because Mr Stelling thinks the boys dislike him, and they want to talk about him behind his back
d) Because Mr Stelling wants the boys to relax and be friends, and they will not do so while adults are present

Answer: ___

Q8. What was Philip doing while Tom went to the fire to warm himself?

a) Philip was drawing objects on a piece of paper
b) Philip was sitting doing nothing at all
c) Philip was walking to the other end of the room
d) Philip was studying his art books

Answer: ___

Q9. What is another word for the adjective "conspicuous" in line 22?

a) Concert
b) Constantly
c) Obvious
d) Considerate

Answer: ___

Q10. What type of words are these from the text: "wrappings", "gentleman", "aversion", "repugnance"?

a) Adjectives
b) Proper nouns
c) Common nouns
d) Pronouns

Answer: ___

Q11. What is the object of this sentence: "Philip was at once too proud and too timid to walk towards Tom."?

a) Philip
b) Tom
c) Walk
d) At once

Answer: ___

Q12. "Tom had a vague notion that the deformity of Wakem's son had some relation to the lawyer's rascality." Which of the following options is closest in meaning to this sentence?

a) Tom felt that Philip had inherited his disability from his father
b) Tom thought that Philip's brutal father had caused his injury in the past
c) Tom felt that Philip's relations had all contributed to Philip's physical problems
d) Tom thought that Philip's disability had something to do with his father being a bad man

Answer: ___

Q13. "Which word means the same as "unamiable" in line 39"?

a) Unanimous
b) Unpleasant
c) Charming
d) Unity

Answer: ___

Q14. How did Philip come to have a disability?

a) He was born with his disability
b) He had recently had a bad fall downstairs
c) He had been in a car crash
d) He had an accident as a child

Answer: ___

Q15. Which of these clauses contains a simile?

a) "The brown hair round it waved and curled at the ends like a girl's…"
b) "…his tongue being completely loosed by surprise and admiration."
c) "This Wakem was a pale, puny fellow…"
d) "Never learned? said Tom, in amazement."

Answer: ___

Q16. What did Philip draw that impressed Tom?

a) A man with a donkey and a dog in a cornfield
b) A monkey, some birds and a spaniel with panniers
c) A donkey with panniers, a spaniel and partridges in the corn
d) Houses, chimneys and windows

Answer: ___

Q17. Tom said he was to learn drawing "this half". What does "this half" mean?

a) This half-day
b) This half-hour
c) This year
d) This school term

Answer: ___

Q18. How many pronouns are in this sentence: "Tom thought he should rather like to show Philip that he had better not try his spiteful tricks on him"?

a) Three

b) Four
c) Five
d) None

Answer: ___

Q19. The same punctuation mark follows all these words in the extract: "him", "thought", "distinctions", "face", "test". What is this punctuation mark called?

a) A hyphen
b) A full stop
c) A semicolon
d) A colon

Answer: ___

Q20. What would Tom have done if anyone had said Tom's father was not a good man?

a) He would have fought them
b) He would have thanked them
c) He would have laughed at them
d) He would have agreed with them

Answer: ___

Q21. Which of these statements is true as evidenced in the text?

a) Tom would rather have had no companion than study with Philip
b) Tom was very happy to have Philip as a study companion
c) Tom would rather study with Philip than have no companion
d) Tom would rather study on his own with no companion at all

Answer: ___

Q22. What parts of animals does Tom find "won't come right" when he tries to draw them?

a) The legs and the tails
b) The heads and the bodies
c) The heads and the legs

d) The legs and the bodies

Answer: ___

Q23. Why do you think the writer has put inverted commas round the expression 'knock under'?

a) Because the writer has invented the phrase and wants to draw attention to it
b) Because the writer is using inverted commas instead of italics to emphasise the phrase
c) Because the writer considers it a slang expression
d) Because the writer does not know what the expression means

Answer: ___

Q24. What is the meaning of the adverb "confidentially" as used in the text at line 75?

a) In a confident way
b) In a way meant to be secret and private
c) In a way meant for everyone to hear
d) In a loud, angry way

Answer: ___

Q25. The disabled tailor Tom disliked was in the neighbourhood of where?

a) Mr Jacob's Academy
b) St Ogg's School
c) Mr Wakem's business
d) The Mill On The Floss

Answer: ___

Q26. Most of this extract is written in the same tense. Which tense is it?

a) The present tense
b) The past tense
c) The pop-up tense
d) The future tense

Q27. The writer describes Philip as having a "melancholy" face. What does this tell us about Philip?

a) Philip has an arrogant, sneering face
b) Philip has a blank, childish face
c) Philip has a jolly, rosy face
d) Philip has a sad, careworn face

Answer: ___

Q28. "O you can do them without learning" said Philip." Which word is the preposition in this sentence?

a) Without
b) You
c) Them
d) Philip

Answer: ___

Q29. Which adjective does *not* describe Philip?

a) Sensitive
b) Proud
c) Aggressive
d) Artistic

Answer: ___

Q30. The "Propriae quae maribus" is a set of grammar rules for which language?

a) Italian
b) Greek
c) Latin
d) German

Answer: ___

Paper Eight: The Mill on the Floss

Q31. "This Wakem was a pale, puny fellow, and it was quite clear he would not be able to play at anything worth speaking of" describes Tom's thoughts about Philip. This sentence contains an example of:

a) Personification
b) Understatement
c) Onomatopoeia
d) Alliteration

Answer: ___

Q32. Tom does not wish to be "too frank about the imperfection of his accomplishments". This means:

a) Tom does not wish to be as imperfect as his friend Frank is
b) Tom does not want to fully admit how imperfectly he does things
c) Tom does not wish people to know how very accomplished he can be
d) Tom wishes to frankly accomplish imperfection

Answer: ___

Q33. What would be another word for "complacency" at line 80?

a) Smugness
b) Sleepiness
c) Complain
d) Commonplace

Answer: ___

Q34. What adjectives best describe Tom's attitude to disability?

a) Understanding and supportive
b) Fearful and ignorant
c) Spiteful and teasing
d) Confused but caring

Answer: ___

Q35. "Tom was quite warm now, and wanted something new to be going forward." How many adjectives are in this sentence?

a) None
b) One
c) Two
d) Three

Answer: ___

Q36. Why might Philip regard Tom's comparative stupidity as "promising"?

a) Because it promises to cause his tutor, Mr Stelling, a lot of problems
b) Because Philip thinks Tom will promise to do better at his lessons
c) Because it promises to put Philip at the top of the class
d) Because it promises to bring Philip some funny moments which will amuse him

Answer: ___

Q37. What kind of words are these from the text: "readily", "heartily", "sideways", "falsely", "towards"?

a) Conjunctions
b) Adverbs
c) Adjectives
d) Proper nouns

Answer: ___

Q38. Which sentence contains a metaphor?

a) He had seen Philip Wakem at St Ogg's, but had always turned his eyes away from him as quickly as possible.
b) "You already know something of each other, I imagine – for you are neighbours at home."
c) Philip, you perceive, was not without a wish to impress the well-made barbarian with a sense of his mental superiority.
d) "O my buttons! I wish I could draw like that."

Answer: ___

Q39. What is the odd word out here: "ill-natured", "puzzled", "inclination", "uncomfortable", "bitter", "furtive"?

a) Puzzled
b) Inclination
c) Furtive
d) Ill-natured

Answer: ___

Q40. Which statement sums up best the relationship between Tom and Philip at this first meeting?

a) Tom dislikes Philip because he is cleverer than Tom and better at drawing. Philip dislikes Tom because he knows Tom's father hates his own father.
b) Philip and Tom get on very well because both boys are equally clever, talented and good at sports.
c) Tom already dislikes Philip because his father hates Philip's father, and Tom is frightened by disability. Philip is wary of Tom and thinks him stupid.
d) Philip hopes that he and Tom will become best friends; but Tom is jealous when he sees Philip is cleverer and more artistic than himself.

Answer: ___

Paper Eight: Answers & Guidance

Q1. This extract begins with Tom's tutor welcoming him back to school. What is the tutor's name?

a) Stephen Ogg
b) Philip Wakem
c) Mr Stelling
d) Mr Jacobs

Answer: C

A straightforward question to begin with, as ever. This is a simple retrieval test, and by looking at the first sentence of the extract we can see that the tutor who welcomed Tom back to school was Mr Stelling, so option **(c)** is the correct answer.

Q2. What two things were awaiting Tom in the study?

a) A bright fire and a hot drink
b) A bright fire and a new companion
c) A comfortable chair and a bright fire
d) A hot drink and a new companion

Answer: B

This is also a retrieval question, but here we are looking for two things. All the options are plausible, as any of them could be in the study, but we need to read lines 2-3 where we find: "You'll find a bright fire there and a new companion." So the right answer is (b).

Q3. A "comforter" was an old word for a…

a) Scarf
b) Glove
c) Leather boot
d) Cup of tea

Answer: A

A vocabulary question which asks us to find the meaning of a word that is no longer in use for something one wears. As usual, if we don't recognise the word, we need to check the context of it within the passage in order to get to the most likely answer. We see at lines 4-5 the sentence: "Tom… took off his woollen comforter and other wrappings." It's clear that neither a leather boot nor a cup of tea would be made of wool, so we can safely reject answers (c) and (d).

A glove could of course be woollen, but then why would a comforter be expressed in the singular rather than the plural? We take gloves off, not just a glove, and there has been no mention in the text of Tom removing one "comforter" previously. So the evidence shows us that (b) is wrong, and the correct answer is thus (a), a scarf – probably the most likely woollen garment to "comfort" someone in cold weather.

Q4. "Tom did not see how a bad man's son could be very good." Which of the following statements best describes Tom's opinion?

a) A bad man's son could be very good
b) A good man's son is always good
c) A good man's son could be very bad
d) A bad man's son could not be very good

Answer: D

This is a question which asks us to paraphrase a sentence from the excerpt. "Paraphrase" means to put something in other, more simple words, and shows the examiner that you have understood the meaning of the text. All the answers here are rather ridiculous, even the correct one, since we know there are no such rules for "good" and "bad" fathers and sons. But we are in Tom's mind, thinking like Tom, and he has some odd ideas. He is prepared to find Philip "bad" simply because his father says Philip's father is a bad man, so **(d)** is the right answer as it explains how Tom thinks.

Q5. Tom was embarrassed as he followed Mr Stelling into the study. What other emotion did he feel?

   a) **Delight**
   b) **Defiance**
   c) **Confusion**
   d) **Destiny**

Answer: B

In lines 9-10 we see that Tom was "in a state of mingled embarrassment and defiance as he followed Mr Stelling to the study." However, we might already have discarded **(a)** as an emotion Tom was certainly not feeling then, and **(d)** because "destiny" is not an emotion; it means fate.

Tom *was* confused in a way, as his emotions were "mingled", but close reading of the text shows us that **(b)** is a stronger answer, that better corresponds with the text.

Q6. What is the meaning of "to make acquaintance" in lines 12-13?

   a) **To join in a game**
   b) **To get to know one another**
   c) **To become best friends**
   d) **To study lessons together**

Answer: B

"To make acquaintance" means to meet and get to know someone, usually at the first time you encounter them. When you know someone slightly, you may call them an acquaintance; they (with luck) become a friend when you know them better. The correct answer here is therefore (**b**).

Q7. Why does the writer use the adverb "wisely" of Mr Stelling's exit from the study in line 18?

   a) Because Mr Stelling is always wise in everything he does, so he even leaves the room wisely
   b) Because Mr Stelling thinks the boys will fight, so he wisely leaves the room as he doesn't want to be involved
   c) Because Mr Stelling thinks the boys dislike him, and they want to talk about him behind his back
   d) Because Mr Stelling wants the boys to relax and be friends, and they will not do so while adults are present

Answer: D

The author diverges from the past tense here and seems to address the reader personally in the present tense. This tells us that he is identifying with the opinion of the character Mr Stelling, who believes that the boys should be left alone to conquer their shyness with one another. We already know the tutor is ignorant of the feud between the fathers of the boys, since he has cheerfully mentioned in line 14 that they probably know each other as neighbours already. Here, he is "wisely" encouraging them to talk to each other in the absence of adults. So (**d**) is the right answer.

Q8. What was Philip doing while Tom went to the fire to warm himself?

   a) Philip was drawing objects on a piece of paper
   b) Philip was sitting doing nothing at all
   c) Philip was walking to the other end of the room
   d) Philip was studying his art books

Paper Eight: Answers & Guidance

183

Answer: A

At lines 23-26 we can find the answer to this retrieval question: "...Tom went to the fire and warmed himself, every now and then casting furtive (meaning hidden or secret) glances at Philip, who seemed to be drawing absently first one object and then another on a piece of paper he had before him." Therefore **(a)** is the correct answer here.

Q9. What is another word for the adjective "conspicuous" in line 22?

a) Concert
b) Constantly
c) Obvious
d) Considerate

Answer: C

As usual, if the word is not familiar, we go back to the context to see where and how the word was used. We see that Philip's disability "...was more conspicuous when he walked." The word is an adjective, describing his disability, so we can immediately reject answer **(a)** "concert" because it is a noun, not an adjective. **(b)** is an adverb, meaning "all the time" so it must be similarly ignored.

(d) *is* an adjective, meaning thoughtful and caring, but could not apply to an abstract noun like disability. We are left with the right answer, **(c)** which fits well, because Philip is sensitive about his limp, so does not want to walk across the room to greet Tom.

Q10. What type of words are these from the text: "wrappings", "gentleman", "aversion", "repugnance"?

a) Adjectives
b) Proper nouns
c) Common nouns
d) Pronouns

Answer: C

All these words are nouns and refer to things, people or emotions. They are common nouns rather than proper nouns, which would require a capital letter. So the correct option here is **(c)**.

Q11. What is the object of this sentence: "Philip was at once too proud and too timid to walk towards Tom."?

a) Philip
b) Tom
c) Walk
d) At once

Answer: B

As we have seen in previous papers, the subject of the sentence is the active "doer" and the object is the more passive "done to" part of the construction of a sentence. So the answer here is **(b)** Tom.

Q12. "Tom had a vague notion that the deformity of Wakem's son had some relation to the lawyer's rascality." Which of the following options is closest in meaning to this sentence?

a) Tom felt that Philip had inherited his disability from his father
b) Tom thought that Philip's brutal father had caused his injury in the past
c) Tom felt that Philip's relations had all contributed to Philip's physical problems
d) Tom thought that Philip's disability had something to do with his father being a bad man

Answer: D

This is another question that asks us to paraphrase a section of the text to show we understand its meaning. The sentence involved is another of Tom's mistaken ideas; not only does he think Philip must be bad because his father is bad, but he has an extraordinary, although "vague", belief that Philip became disabled simply because his father was a rascal. So **(d)** is the correct answer.

Q13. "Which word means the same as "unamiable" in line 39"?

a) **Unanimous**
b) **Unpleasant**
c) **Charming**
d) **Unity**

Answer: B

Another vocabulary question – we know what to do unless we happen to be familiar with the word already: check the context and the part of speech to ensure they make sense.

"Unamiable" is an adjective which cannot have the same meaning as a noun, so option **(d)**, the noun "unity", must be rejected. **(a)** "Unanimous" means in full agreement, not relevant to describe someone's character. Charming has the opposite meaning to the correct one, and children would probably not be rudely "hooting" at someone charming, so **(c)** must go too, leaving us with the appropriate, and correct, answer **(b)**.

Q14. How did Philip come to have a disability?

a) **He was born with his disability**
b) **He had recently had a bad fall downstairs**
c) **He had been in a car crash**
d) **He had an accident as a child**

Answer: D

It is not very likely that Philip would have been in a car crash, since the text was written in 1860, before cars were invented. The other options are possible, but at lines 31-32 we learn that "...the deformity of Philip's spine was not a congenital (meaning "from birth") hump, but the result of an accident in infancy." So we can confirm that **(d)** is the best answer.

Q15. Which of these clauses contains a simile?

   a) "The brown hair round it waved and curled at the ends like a girl's..."
   b) "...his tongue being completely loosed by surprise and admiration."
   c) "This Wakem was a pale, puny fellow..."
   d) "Never learned? said Tom, in amazement."

Answer: A

A simile contains a comparison of one thing to another, using the words "like", "as" or "as if". The only answer including a construction like this is **(a)**, which is the correct answer.

Q16. What did Philip draw that impressed Tom?

   a) A man with a donkey and a dog in a cornfield
   b) A monkey, some birds and a spaniel with panniers
   c) A donkey with panniers, a spaniel and partridges in the corn
   d) Houses, chimneys and windows

Answer: C

The answer is in the text, but all the answers contain items mentioned in the text, so it is useful to look back and select the exact options. At line 54 we read Tom's exclamation: "Why, that's a donkey with panniers (baskets on its saddle) – and a spaniel, and partridges in the corn!" So the correct answer is **(c)**. Answer **(d)** is what Tom himself, *not* Philip, claimed to be able to draw.

• • •

Q17. Tom said he was to learn drawing "this half". What does "this half" mean?

a) This half-day
b) This half-hour
c) This year
d) This school term

Answer: D

Options (**a**) and (**b**) can be excluded immediately; even a genius (and we know Tom is not one of those) could not learn to draw in a half-hour or a half-day. Option (**c**) seems possible, but why would a year be referred to as "a half"? The most likely amount of time here is option (**d**) and it is the right one. School years used to be split into two, and were called "halves" as in "half-years". Some schools and colleges still use a "half" instead of the word "term".

Q18. How many pronouns are in this sentence: "Tom thought he should rather like to show Philip that he had better not try his spiteful tricks on him"?

a) Three
b) Four
c) Five
d) None

Answer: B

Pronouns, as we have learnt, are short words used instead of nouns, when using the noun every time would be repetitive and ugly to read or speak aloud. If we did not use pronouns, the sentence in this question would be "...Tom thought Tom should rather like to show Philip that Philip had better not try his spiteful tricks on Tom." That is ungainly and unnecessary. So, in the original sentence we can count "he" twice, "his" once and "him" also once, making four pronouns altogether; therefore the right answer is (**b**).

. . .

Q19. The same punctuation mark follows all these words in the extract: "him", "thought", "distinctions", "face", "test". What is this punctuation mark called?

   a) A hyphen
   b) A full stop
   c) A semicolon
   d) A colon

Answer: D

This punctuation question could be quite demanding, as it might require a skip through the entire text, making a note of the specified words and the punctuation mark following them. We find that all the words precede a colon, so the correct answer is (**d**).

Colons are useful before dialogue, lists, or explanations. They can also give emphasis to an idea already expressed, as in the sentence at lines 32-34: "...but you do not expect from Tom any acquaintance with such distinctions: to him, Philip was simply a humpback."

Q20. What would Tom have done if anyone had said Tom's father was not a good man?

   a) He would have fought them
   b) He would have thanked them
   c) He would have laughed at them
   d) He would have agreed with them

Answer: A

More retrieval, this time from the text at lines 8-9: "[Tom's] own father was a good man, and he would readily have fought any one who said the contrary." So we can see the right answer is (**a**). All the other options are very unlikely, knowing Tom's personality as it is written in this extract.

. . .

Paper Eight: Answers & Guidance

Q21. Which of these statements is true as evidenced in the text?

a) Tom would rather have had no companion than study with Philip
b) Tom was very happy to have Philip as a study companion
c) Tom would rather study with Philip than have no companion
d) Tom would rather study on his own with no companion at all

Answer: C

If we reread lines 47-50 we can find the answer to this question. In Tom's thoughts "It was certainly more agreeable to have an ill-natured humpback as a companion than to stand looking out of the study window at the rain and kicking his foot against the washboard in solitude..." Tom's nature is such that he dislikes being alone and would rather have even someone he didn't like, than nobody at all with whom to study. So the correct answer is **(c)**.

Q22. What parts of animals does Tom find "won't come right" when he tries to draw them?

a) The legs and the tails
b) The heads and the bodies
c) The heads and the legs
d) The legs and the bodies

Answer: C

In lines 59-60 Tom says: "Why, when I make dogs and horses and those things, the heads and legs won't come right..." Therefore we know the right option here is **(c)**.

Q23. Why do you think the writer has put inverted commas round the expression 'knock under'?

a) Because the writer has invented the phrase and wants to draw attention to it

b) Because the writer is using inverted commas instead of italics to emphasise the phrase
c) Because the writer considers it a slang expression
d) Because the writer does not know what the expression means

Answer: C

A slightly more tricky question here. Inverted commas can be used for many reasons, but emphasis is not one of them: italics, underlining, capitals, colons and exclamation marks all fulfil that function in different circumstances. So we can reject answer (**b**). Nor do inverted commas mean the expression is invented by the writer and are needed to draw attention to it, so (**a**) is wrong too. A writer would hardly use an expression at all if he did not know what it meant, so answer (**d**) should be dismissed with the other two.

"Knock under" means to admit defeat, to accept your weakness or failure, and at the time the book was written it was a schoolboy slang expression which the writer is using in a slightly ironic way. So the answer (**c**) is again correct!

Q24. What is the meaning of the adverb "confidentially" as used in the text at line 75?

a) In a confident way
b) In a way meant to be secret and private
c) In a way meant for everyone to hear
d) In a loud, angry way

Answer: B

Again, if the meaning of the word in a vocabulary question is not known, we should go through the options and the context to make our decision. Firstly, "confident" and "confidential" are not the same word nor have the same meaning, so (**a**) is wrong.

(**c**) and (**d**) are contradicted by the context of the word: Tom is "lowering his voice confidentially" so he would hardly be likely to want everyone to hear (particularly his tutor, given what he is saying) and he could not be lowering his voice if he was speaking loudly and angrily. So we come to (**b**), which makes sense here and is the right answer. If one speaks confidentially, one only wants the person one is directly addressing to hear what one says.

Q25. The disabled tailor Tom disliked was in the neighbourhood of where?

 a) Mr Jacob's Academy
 b) St Ogg's School
 c) Mr Wakem's business
 d) The Mill On The Floss

Answer: A

A retrieval question which can be solved by checking line 38 in the extract: "There was a humpbacked tailor in the neighbourhood of Mr Jacob's Academy..." So the right option here is (**a**).

Q26. Most of this extract is written in the same tense. Which tense is it?

 a) The present tense
 b) The past tense
 c) The pop-up tense
 d) The future tense

Answer: B

Apart from an occasional departure into the present tense so the writer can address the reader more directly, or during the characters' speech, most of the narrative is in the past tense, so the answer is (**b**). There is no such thing as the "pop-up tense"; it is a red herring – a bad pun on "pop-up tents", the tents that assemble themselves by expanding automatically!

Q27. The writer describes Philip as having a "melancholy" face. What does this tell us about Philip?

a) **Philip has an arrogant, sneering face**
b) **Philip has a blank, childish face**
c) **Philip has a jolly, rosy face**
d) **Philip has a sad, careworn face**

Answer: D

There is nothing in the text about Philip being arrogant or sneering; in fact Philip mostly hides his emotions and takes care not to laugh at Tom. So (**a**) seems very unlikely, as does (**b**) since we read at line 29 that Philip's face is comparatively "old-looking" compared to Tom's, so it is not blank and childish at all. Having a "jolly, rosy" face does not fit Philip's character or physique as delineated in the extract, so we can reject (**c**) too.

"Melancholy" is an adjective meaning sad and thoughtful by nature, so if we factor in the description of Philip looking old for his years, we can deduce that the correct answer is (**d**).

Q28. "O you can do them without learning" said Philip." Which word is the preposition in this sentence?

a) **Without**
b) **You**
c) **Them**
d) **Philip**

Answer: A

Prepositions are words which can be used to define relationships between different parts of a sentence that may refer to a time, place, direction etc. "You" and "Them" are pronouns, and "Philip" is a proper noun, as it is a person's given name and thus begins with a capital letter. So we are left with answer (**a**) which is the right one.

Q29. Which adjective does *not* describe Philip?

a) **Sensitive**

b) Proud
c) Aggressive
d) Artistic

Answer: C

An "odd-one-out" clue again here. The personalities of both boys are brought out very clearly in this extract, and we may see the right option immediately and have no need to eliminate the wrong ones. However, as usual if there is any doubt, we can find evidence in the text to confirm our choice.

At line 81 we see that Philip does not want to openly laugh at Tom, as he is "made polite by his own extreme sensitiveness". So as we have proof that Philip is indeed sensitive, we can rule out answer (**a**). Is Philip proud? At line 20 we read "Philip was at once too proud and too timid to walk towards Tom". So he has pride too, and (**b**) can thus be rejected.

We know that Philip can draw very well, as his art provokes "admiration" from Tom, who is very much prepared to dislike him, so (**d**) must go too, leaving us with (**c**).

Does Philip show aggressive tendencies? We have already learnt he is "timid", in fact the writer uses the adjective twice of Philip, in line 15 as well as in our previous example. Aggression is usually loud and violent, and Philip is described as "pale and puny", besides which he has an opportunity to make Tom feel bad when Tom exposes his ignorance of Latin, yet Philip declines to make any hurtful comments. Aggression seems to have no part in his character, so we can be sure that answer (**c**) is the correct one.

Q30. The "Propriae quae maribus" is a set of grammar rules for which language?

a) Italian
b) Greek
c) Latin
d) German

Answer: C

We do not need to understand or be able to translate Latin to recognise the language when we see it written. In fact this book of grammar did exist: in English it was known as "The Posing Of The Rules" and was written by William Lily in the sixteenth century as a beginner's guide to the gender of Latin nouns. Even if we did not recognise it, we can tell the correct answer is **(c)**, because the boys are discussing learning Latin rather than any of the other languages.

Q31. "This Wakem was a pale, puny fellow, and it was quite clear he would not be able to play at anything worth speaking of" describes Tom's thoughts about Philip. This sentence contains an example of:

a) **Personification**
b) **Understatement**
c) **Onomatopoeia**
d) **Alliteration**

Answer: D

An alliteration, as we have seen, is when two or more words together, or close together, begin with the same letter. The adjectives "pale" and "puny" (meaning weak) next to each other in the sentence make **(d)** the right option here.

Q32. Tom does not wish to be "too frank about the imperfection of his accomplishments". This means:

a) **Tom does not wish to be as imperfect as his friend Frank is**
b) **Tom does not want to fully admit how imperfectly he does things**
c) **Tom does not wish people to know how very accomplished he can be**
d) **Tom wishes to frankly accomplish imperfection**

Answer: B

A question which not only asks us to paraphrase a clause, but includes a bit of a vocabulary testing too. "Accomplishments" as used here are things that one has achieved in life, and Tom's accomplishments are apparently imperfect. However, he does not want Philip to know too much about his weaknesses, so he says rather braggingly "I daresay I could [draw] dogs and horses if I were to try more" in order to lessen the effect of all the genuine praise he gave to Philip's artwork and appear more talented himself. The nearest meaning to the quoted clause is answer **(b)**.

Q33. What would be another word for "complacency" at line 80?

a) Smugness
b) Sleepiness
c) Complain
d) Commonplace

Answer: A

Complacency is a noun, described in the text by the adjective "bitter". "Complain" is a verb, and "commonplace" is an adjective (meaning dull and routine) so we can quickly dismiss answers **(c)** and **(d)**.

Sleepiness is a noun, but when we look at the context of the word we see that "Philip felt some bitter sleepiness in the promising stupidity..." would be nonsense, so **(b)** must be wrong too.

Complacency means a feeling of satisfaction with oneself, or smugness, so **(a)** is the correct answer here. Philip feels smug, because he knows he is cleverer and further ahead in his studies than Tom. But there is a "bitter" feeling to it as well, because he would like to be as healthy and sporty as Tom, and he doesn't really enjoy his "complacency" because he is self-aware and he knows smugness is not a positive emotion to feel.

Q34. What adjectives best describe Tom's attitude to disability?

a) Understanding and supportive
b) Fearful and ignorant
c) Spiteful and teasing
d) Confused but caring

Answer: B

Although Tom has a regrettably ill-informed attitude to disability (obvious physical disability was often called "deformity" when this text was written), he is not spiteful and does not tease Philip on account of his spinal problem. So we can exclude answer **(c)** here.

Unfortunately, though, Tom could not be called "caring", "supportive" or "understanding", so we must also reject answers **(a)** and **(d)**.

There are plenty of examples of Tom's ignorance about disability – his belief that Philip is disabled because his father is a bad man, and his "puzzled suspicion that Philip's crooked back might be the source of remarkable faculties"; in other words, Tom was prepared to believe that Philip's disability caused his artistic talent! These examples show his ignorance, and at lines 36-37 we can see that Tom "felt too a half-admitted fear of [Philip] as probably a spiteful fellow, who, not being able to fight you, had cunning ways of doing you a mischief by the sly." So ignorance in Tom has bred fear too, making the correct answer to this question option **(b)**.

Q35. "Tom was quite warm now, and wanted something new to be going forward." How many adjectives are in this sentence?

 a) None
 b) One
 c) Two
 d) Three

Answer: C

There are two adjectives in this sentence: "warm" and "new". Therefore **(c)** is the right option here. If we had any confusion about "quite" before "warm", it is an adverb of degree.

Q36. Why might Philip regard Tom's comparative stupidity as "promising"?

 a) Because it promises to cause his tutor, Mr Stelling, a lot of problems.

b) Because Philip thinks Tom will promise to do better at his lessons.
c) Because it promises to put Philip at the top of the class.
d) Because it promises to bring Philip some funny moments which will amuse him

Answer: D

We are looking for the best answer here, as there is no direct explanation within the text. Examining answer (**a**) we see there is no proof in the extract that Philip dislikes Mr Stelling or wants to upset him, so we can discard that option. Answer (**b**) is random – Philip has shown no interest in whether Tom does better or not. Answer (**c**) is a possibility, except that we have had no evidence to show that Philip cares about being at the top of the class, whereas with the final answer we *do* have evidence that Philip is amused by Tom's stupidity, even though he "checked his inclination to laugh". So the best answer here is (**d**).

Q37. What kind of words are these from the text: "readily", "heartily", "sideways", "falsely", "towards"?

a) Conjunctions
b) Adverbs
c) Adjectives
d) Proper nouns

Answer: B

These words are all adverbs. The ones ending "ly" are adverbs of manner; "sideways" and "towards" are adverbs of place. So (**b**) is correct.

Q38. Which sentence contains a metaphor?

a) He had seen Philip Wakem at St Ogg's, but had always turned his eyes away from him as quickly as possible.
b) "You already know something of each other, I imagine – for you are neighbours at home."

c) **Philip, you perceive, was not without a wish to impress the well-made barbarian with a sense of his mental superiority.**
c) **"O my buttons! I wish I could draw like that."**

Answer: C

A metaphor, as mentioned before, is a comparison of one thing to another – and although a simile (a comparison that makes use of the phrase "like" or "as") is technically a type of metaphor, for the sake of 11+ exams, it is probably best to consider them as two separate things.

The right answer here is **(c)** because when the writer says "barbarian" he means Tom. Tom of course is not really a brutish or savage person who comes from outside a great classical civilisation, as the word barbarian meant originally. Tom's health, physical strength, and sheer ignorance make Philip think of him as a barbarian, and thus the writer encapsulates in one word the impression Tom has made on Philip.

Q39. What is the odd word out here: "ill-natured", "puzzled", "inclination", "uncomfortable", "bitter", "furtive"?

a) **Puzzled**
b) **Inclination**
c) **Furtive**
d) **Ill-natured**

Answer: B

A last "odd-one-out" question as we come to the end of the paper. All these words from the extract are adjectives, except for "inclination" (meaning a natural tendency), which is a common abstract noun. So the word which is different to the others is option **(b)**.

Q40. Which statement sums up best the relationship between Tom and Philip at this first meeting?

a) **Tom dislikes Philip because he is cleverer than Tom and better**

at drawing. Philip dislikes Tom because he knows Tom's father hates his own father.
b) Philip and Tom get on very well because both boys are equally clever, talented and good at sports.
c) Tom already dislikes Philip because his father hates Philip's father, and Tom is frightened by disability. Philip is wary of Tom and thinks him stupid.
d) Philip hopes that he and Tom will become best friends; but Tom is jealous when he sees Philip is cleverer and more artistic than himself.

Answer: C

The final question here is a broader one, to show that we have understood a thread which runs through the whole narrative, rather than simply being able to retrieve specific ideas or words from the text.

Answer **(a)** first says Tom dislikes Philip because Philip is cleverer and more talented than him. We know this is not true – even before Tom saw Philip's drawings, he disliked him because of his father's prejudice and Tom's own fear of disability. Philip as far as we know is unaware of Tom's father's hatred, so the second part of option **(a)** is also incorrect.

Option **(b)** is even less true to the text – the boys are opposites in their tastes, their natures and their intellects. So we can reject it completely.

Option **(d)** suggests that Philip thinks Tom and he will be best friends, but there is absolutely no support for that in the extract, and nor is there any jealousy from Tom about Philip's drawings – in fact Tom is surprised into praising the artwork despite his dislike of Philip. So we must forget this option too, and look at the only one left.

Option **(c)** sums up the relationship between the boys better than any other. We have seen how Tom has been influenced by his father's "hot emphasis" on Philip's father's bad behaviour, so he is prepared to dislike Philip from the outset. We also know Tom is nervous about disability because he ignorantly equates it to slyness and spitefulness of character. Philip is wary of Tom and in line 27 was "trying to overcome his own repugnance (meaning loathing) to making the first advances." Philip is intensely sensitive about his disability and is wary of meeting new people; in line 20-21 we learn that "He thought, or rather felt, that Tom had an aversion to looking at him." Finally, we know that Philip finds Tom has "promising stupidity". With all this evidence from the text, we can be confident in knowing the right answer to the last question is option **(c)**.

Afterword

If you found this book useful, please consider leaving a review on Amazon.

You can also join our private Facebook group (where our authors share resources and guidance) by visiting the following link: https://rcl.ink/UM7b9

Accolade Press for Entrance Exams

https://accoladetuition.com/accolade-preschool-primary

7+

7+ Comprehension: Practice Papers & In-Depth Guided Answers

7+ Comprehension: Practice Papers & In-Depth Guided Answers: Volume 2

11+

11+ Creative Writing: A Technique Guide

11+ Comprehension: Practice Papers & In-Depth Guided Answers

11+ Comprehension: Practice Papers & In-Depth Guided Answers: Volume 2

11+ Multiple-Choice Comprehension: Practice Papers & In-Depth Guided Answers

Accolade Press for Key Stage 2 & 3

https://accoladetuition.com/accolade-preschool-primary

Creative Writing for KS2: The Ultimate Technique Guide & Workbook

Creative Writing For KS3: A Technique Guide

English Literature for KS3: A Complete Guide

Accolade Press for GCSE English: The Range

www.accoladetuition.com/accolade-gcse-guides

English Literature

Romeo and Juliet: Essay Writing Guide for GCSE (9-1)

Macbeth: Essay Writing Guide for GCSE (9-1)

Power and Conflict: Essay Writing Guide for GCSE (9-1)

Dr Jekyll and Mr Hyde: Essay Writing Guide for GCSE (9-1)

A Christmas Carol: Essay Writing Guide for GCSE (9-1)

The Merchant of Venice: Essay Writing Guide for GCSE (9-1)

Love and Relationships: Essay Writing Guide for GCSE (9-1)

Great Expectations: Essay Writing Guide for GCSE (9-1)

An Inspector Calls: Essay Writing Guide for GCSE (9-1)

Pride and Prejudice: Essay Writing Guide for GCSE (9-1)

The Tempest: Essay Writing Guide for GCSE (9-1)

Unseen Poetry: Essay Writing Guide for GCSE (9-1)

Much Ado About Nothing: Essay Writing Guide for GCSE (9-1)

Lord of the Flies: Essay Writing Guide for GCSE (9-1)

English Language

English Language Paper One: A Technique Guide for GCSE (9-1)

English Language Paper Two : A Technique Guide for GCSE (9-1)

www.ingramcontent.com/pod-product-compliance
Lightning Source LLC
Chambersburg PA
CBHW081347080526
44588CB00016B/2399